CONTENTS

❄

Good Housekeeping

THE GREAT CHRISTMAS COOKIE SWAP COOKBOOK

60 Large-Batch Recipes to Bake and Share

HEARST BOOKS

A division of Sterling Publishing Co., Inc.

New York / London
www.sterlingpublishing.com

GOOD HOUSEKEEPING

Rosemary Ellis   Editor in Chief
Susan Westmoreland   Food Director
Samantha Cassetty   Nutrition Director
Sharon Franke   Food Appliance Director

Book design by Jan Derevjanik

10 9 8 7 6 5 4 3 2 1

The Good Housekeeping Cookbook Seal guarantees that the recipes
in this cookbook meet the strict standards of the Good
Housekeeping Research Institute. The Institute has been a source
of reliable information and a consumer advocate since 1900, and
established its seal of approval in 1909. Every recipe has been
triple-tested for ease, reliability, and great taste.

Published by Hearst Books
A division of Sterling Publishing Co., Inc.
387 Park Avenue South, New York, NY 10016

Good Housekeeping is a trademark of Hearst Communications, Inc.

www.goodhousekeeping.com

For information about custom editions, special sales, premium and
corporate purchases, please contact Sterling Special Sales
Department at 800-805-5489 or
specialsales@sterlingpublishing.com.

Distributed in Canada by Sterling Publishing
c/o Canadian Manda Group, 165 Dufferin Street
Toronto, Ontario, Canada M6K 3H6

Distributed in Australia by Capricorn Link (Australia) Pty. Ltd.
P.O. Box 704, Windsor, NSW 2756 Australia

This special edition was printed for Kohl's Department Stores, Inc.
(for distribution on behalf of Kohl's Cares, LLC, its wholly owned
subsidiary) by Hearst Books, a division of Sterling Publishing Co., Inc.

Manufactured in China

ISBN 978-1-58816-882-5

share the joy!

The holiday countdown starts early at *Good Housekeeping*. When most people are headed to the beach, we're baking batches of Christmas cookies in the test kitchens. No matter what the calendar says, the aroma of cookies baking brings out a smile from anyone who passes by—and the rest of the magazine staff stops in more frequently than usual. We always reward them with a taste of whatever we are baking, and, in return, many of them have passed on to us their family's favorite cookie recipes.

Sharing the joy of the season with festive foods and sweet indulgences is as much a part of the celebration as the Christmas tree. That's why we've created this special collection of cookie recipes that are just perfect to share with friends and family—and what better way to do that than at a cookie swap?

Here you'll find recipes formulated for large batches of eight dozen cookies or more, for traditional favorites and new taste treats, all guaranteed to delight a crowd of cookie lovers. If you're new to the world of cookie swapping, our helpful hints for organizing one will start you off right, and our baking tips ensure that every batch you bake will be perfect. We've even included blank recipe cards for each participant to write a special memory of details about her cookie, and pass out color copies for each guest to take home with her stash.

We hope this selection inspires you to make cookies—and cookie swapping—a part of your annual holiday tradition.

Susan Westmoreland
Food Director, *Good Housekeeping*

hosting a
great christmas cookie swap

❄

A platter of festive cookies is a hallmark of the holiday season. And yet, each year it seems the holidays become ever more rushed and frantic, leaving one to ask: "Who has time to bake all those cookies?" A Christmas cookie swap (some call it a cookie exchange) offers a way to have a great selection of delicious homemade cookies while allowing for what's truly important: spending time with friends and family.

A cookie swap is easy to host and loads of fun. Here's how it's done.

INVITE YOUR FRIENDS AND FAMILY

Sometime in November—or two to three weeks ahead of your cookie swap date—invite a group of six to ten friends and/or family members to join in the fun. Ask each person to bake and bring one type of cookie to share with the group. Remember, calendars fill up quickly during the holidays, so pick a convenient time (Sunday afternoons are great) and be specific about the start and end time for the party.

The RSVP date on your invitation is important. Your guests will have to tell you what kind of cookie they will bring so that you can make sure there's no duplication and guarantee that everyone will take home a great selection. Allow enough time between the RSVP date and the party for those attending to shop for supplies and bake their cookies.

Once you know how many people will be participating, you can tell your guests how many cookies to bring. There are several ways to do this. You might have each person bring enough cookies for everyone to leave with a small selection, or have each person bring a half- or full dozen cookies for each person attending plus an extra dozen for sampling during the party. Keep things easy and fun—the most important reason for holding a cookie swap is to spend time with family and friends.

❄

REMEMBER THOSE LESS FORTUNATE DURING THE HOLIDAYS: Ask each guest to bake just one more dozen and create a tray or basket for your local shelter, hospital, retirement home, or a family in need.

BEFORE THE SWAP

Make sure each guest brings copies of their recipe to pass around—and if there's a special tradition or family history attached to their cookie, ask the guest to write that information on the recipe. You may find that some are unwilling to share "secret" family recipes. That's okay, but since many people have food allergies, it's important that your guests know the ingredients in the cookies at your party. (Ask your guests in advance if there are allergies in their family and let all the participants know so they can take this into account when choosing their recipes.)

Participants can pre-divide their cookies onto paper plates or disposable containers to bring to the party, but it's more festive to set up a table with all the cookies on individual platters and have guests make their selection. Ask your guests to bring large containers to collect their cookies and carry them home. Have waxed paper on hand for them to separate their cookies as needed.

Someone may want to participate in your cookie swap but be unable to attend the party. Those cookies can be dropped off in advance, and you can make a selection of cookies for the absent friend to pick up at a convenient time.

❄

WHEN BAKING YOUR OWN COOKIES FOR THE SWAP, you may want to consider making an extra batch or two. Inevitably, mishaps occur—a burnt batch, a late-night "cookie raid" by hungry children (or the family dog!), or even a cookie tray dropped while walking from the front door to the car. Your backup batches ensures that everyone gets a full selection of goodies.

PARTY SETUP

Decorate and prepare the area where the cookies are to be displayed: Cover the dining room table, a large coffee table, or a large folding table with a pretty holiday cloth. Have extra platters on hand to lay out the cookies. In a pinch, cardboard box bottoms can be covered with foil for attractive display.

In addition to the cookies you and your guests will be sampling, the party fare can be as simple or elaborate as you like (but do keep the cookies as the main event). Have a selection of beverages available. This is a great time to pull out the punch bowl, too, so think about offering a holiday-themed specialty, with or without alcohol. Salty snacks will also be welcomed to balance the richness of the cookies. And don't forget small plates and napkins.

IT'S SWAP TIME!

As your guests arrive, have them place their cookies in the display area, with copies of the recipes alongside. You'll want to do some socializing before getting down to the business of the swap—enjoy some holiday music and catch up with conversation. If cookie sam-

pling prior to the swap is part of your plan, ask guests to share the story of their cookie, if they have one. Did they use a family recipe; are there fond memories associated with it; or perhaps there's a funny-in-hindsight cookie disaster they'd like to admit?

❄

IF YOU OR YOUR GUESTS HAVE YOUNG CHILDREN, plan an event to keep the little ones occupied during the swap. Enlist a teenager to take them to a movie or to oversee an activity in the den or family room—away from the cookies.

When it's time to swap, each person walks around the cookie display with their container, and takes their fair share of the goodies in whatever amount has been predetermined. Now everyone can share a delicious assortment of homemade cookies with their loved ones—and they only had to bake one kind. And you'll have had so much fun that a cookie swap will surely become an annual tradition. Think of the different ways you can enjoy this type of exchange:

- Have a mother/daughter cookie swap. Invite mothers with their daughters (of any age) to participate as teams. It's a wonderful way for your guests to pass down their family traditions.
- Are you part of a large family? Have each member pick a favorite family cookie recipe to bake and share.
- Invite the neighbors. A cookie swap is a terrific way to foster community and spread holiday cheer.
- Share with your co-workers. Have a lunch-hour cookie swap at the office.
- Take turns hosting each year. Spend this year's swap discussing possible themes for the next one—perhaps a swap featuring international cookie recipes or all-chocolate cookies is in your future.

The themes are endless but the goal is the same: to share the warmth—and minimize the work—of the holiday season.

perfect cookies you'll be proud to share

---- ❄ ----

Nothing smells or tastes better than a batch of cookies hot from the oven, especially when they turn out just the way you want them: moist and chewy or light and crispy. Getting it right is easy if you follow the step-by-step directions with every recipe and use the ingredients and the amounts called for.

Most cookies don't require any fancy equipment. However, there are a few essential baking utensils that can make the difference between a cookie that tastes just so-so and one that's a Wow! So before you start baking, make sure you have the right equipment on hand and that you're using the best ingredients.

THE INGREDIENTS OF SUCCESS

Baking is a precise art. To ensure that your cookies will taste delicious and have just the right texture, it is important to use the exact ingredients called for and to handle them properly.

BUTTER OR MARGARINE? While either one may be used for many cookie recipes, for the best flavor and texture, use butter. If you prefer to use margarine when the recipe gives it as an alternative to butter, make sure it contains 80 percent butter fat. Don't substitute margarine if the recipe calls only for butter. Don't substitute light margarine, vegetable-oil spreads, or whipped butters for stick margarine; they contain more water than standard sticks and won't work in cookies unless the recipes have been formulated especially for these products. See Figgy Bars (page 42), Whole-Grain Gingersnaps (page 124), Whole-Wheat Sugar Cookies (page 84), and Berry-

Orange Linzer Jewels (page 85) for recipes specially formulated to use trans fat–free vegetable oil spreads.

Be sure to soften or chill butter or margarine if the recipe calls for it. Some doughs (like spritz) won't blend properly unless the butter is spoonable; leave it at room temperature until it's very soft and spreadable, but don't melt it (to speed up the process, cut it into small pieces). It's best not to soften butter or margarine in the microwave. This can melt some areas, which can hurt the cookies' texture. For other doughs, like some shortbreads, be aware that if the butter isn't refrigerated, the dough will be too soft and greasy to work with.

TO GREASE COOKIE SHEETS, your best bet is vegetable shortening. Avoid both butter, which browns, and vegetable oil, which leaves a gummy residue on baking pans. Vegetable oil cooking sprays with flour added also works well. Grease cookie sheets only when a recipe directs you to. Some cookies have a high fat content, so greasing isn't necessary.

THE TYPE OF FLOUR IS IMPORTANT. Most cookie recipes call for all-purpose flour. Occasionally, a cookie recipe will call for cake flour, which is lower in protein and gluten and will produce a more tender cookie. Cake and all-purpose flours are not interchangeable, so read your recipe carefully. In either case, make sure the flour you are using is not self-rising.

White whole-wheat flour is a good alternative for those who want to up their whole-grain quotient. Milled from an albino variety of wheat, it's as healthy as traditional whole wheat but it lacks the heartier taste and grainy heft. It's ideal for all whole-grain recipes and can be substituted for up to half of the all-purpose flour in many other recipes without substantially changing the taste. If you can't find white whole wheat flour in your supermarket, you can order it from King Arthur Flour; 800-777-4434 or kingarthurflour.com.

BAKING SODA is a leavening agent that makes cookies rise. Keep the box or tin tightly closed in a cool, dry place so the baking soda stays very active. For best results, replace after six months.

BAKING POWDER is a premeasured mixture of baking soda and an acid. (It takes twice as much baking powder as baking soda to leaven a product.) Again, keep baking powder tightly closed in a cook, dry place and, for best results, replace after six months.

❄

TOASTING NUTS

When cookie recipes call for nuts, we often specify that they be toasted. That's because a few minutes of warmth and a quick shake in the pan bring out the deep, rich flavor of every nut from almonds to pecans. Follow these toasting guidelines for the best (no-burn) results.

Toast nuts whole (without shells), then chop with a chef's knife. If you chop them before toasting, they burn quickly.

1 • Preheat regular or toaster oven to 350°F.

2 • Place nuts in single layer in metal baking pan (not cookie sheet).

3 • Shake pan or stir nuts occasionally. Stir from edge (where they cook more quickly) to center and vice versa; watch carefully and remove from oven as soon as nuts begin to brown.

4 • Immediately transfer to cool plate (otherwise, they'll continue to brown in the hot pan).

To remove the bitter skins from hazelnuts, toast them as directed above until any portions without skin begin to brown. Transfer the nuts to a clean, dry kitchen towel and rub them until the skins come off.

- -

MEASURE BY MEASURE

A pinch of this and a dash of that is a recipe for disaster; measure everything! Unlike soups and stews, where too much or too little of an ingredient blends in without much consequence, cookie recipes are exact formulas, and what you add or subtract could affect the final texture.

Assemble a *mise en place*, the French term for a lineup of pre-measured ingredients, on the counter before you begin. (If you don't want to use and then wash custard cups and bowls, place the dry ingredients on pieces of waxed paper.) This reduces your chances of omitting an ingredient or measuring it incorrectly.

And even though it worked for Grandma, don't use coffee or tea cups or tableware teaspoons and tablespoons for measuring. Use dry measuring cups to measure dry ingredients and liquid measuring cups for wet ingredients; the two kinds of cups don't hold the same volume. Ideally, you should have:

- Set of standard dry-ingredient measuring cups
- Set of standard measuring spoons
- Spatula for leveling them
- 1-cup glass measure for liquids
- 2-cup and 4-cup glass measures for liquids

Always measure ingredients over waxed paper or into an empty bowl, but never over your bowl of already measured ingredients—just in case there is a spill.

LIQUIDS. Use clear glass measuring cups. Place the cup on a level surface and bend down so that your eyes are in line with the marks on the cup.

MEASURE FLOUR: Stir the flour to keep it from packing and spoon it into a standard dry measuring cup. Level the top of the dry measure by passing a metal spatula over the top to remove the excess.

DRY INGREDIENTS. To measure flour and other dry ingredients that tend to pack down in the storage container, stir and then spoon them into a standard dry-ingredient measuring cup. Level the top surface with a spatula, scraping off the excess into a bowl.

GRANULATED SUGAR. Just scoop or pour it into a dry-ingredient measuring cup.

BROWN SUGAR. Pack it into the measuring cup and then level.

BUTTER, VEGETABLE SHORTENING, AND MARGARINE. Tablespoons are marked on the wrapper, so you can just cut off the desired amount using a knife.

SYRUP, HONEY, AND OTHER STICKY INGREDIENTS. Lightly oil the cup first (with vegetable oil) and the ingredient will pour right out without sticking to the cup.

ABOUT MERINGUES

- Don't make meringues on a humid or rainy day; they will absorb too much moisture and turn out soggy.
- Make sure all sugar inthe beaten meringue has dissolved. Test by rubbing a bit of the mixture between your fingers—it should feel smooth, not grainy.
- To give meringues extra crispness and sparkle, sprinkle them with granulated sugar before baking.
- Bake meringues at a low temperature (200° to 275° F) so they dry out thoroughly without overbrowning.
- Let hard meringues dry completely in the turned off oven for crisp results. They will have a gummy texture if removed too soon,
- Hard meringues can be made ahead and stored up to a week in an airtight container.

MIXING IT UP AND SHAPING

While a lot of cookie batters can be stirred up with whatever spoon is on hand, the right equipment makes it easier, particularly if your recipe calls for chopping a lot of nuts or doing a lot of mixing. You should have:

- Stand mixer or hand beater
- Food processor or mini-processor
- Set of mixing bowls: small, medium, and large
- Several wooden spoons for stirring hot ingredients on the stove

Overmixing dough results in tough cookies. Unless a recipe says otherwise, mix dough just until blended after adding flour.

Roll dough on a flat, smooth surface. Work from the center to the edge and cut out as many cookies as possible (rerolled scraps yield tough cookies.) Before rolling dough between 2 sheets of waxed paper, sprinkle work surface with a bit of water to prevent the paper from sliding.

When dropping, shaping, or rolling and cutting dough, try to maintain a uniform size and thickness to ensure even baking. Follow directions exactly for amount of dough used per cookie. If recipe says, "Drop by rounded teaspoons," we mean measuring teaspoons, not spoons used to stir tea. A 1-inch ball should really be 1 inch in diameter; measure one with a ruler to get the idea.

THE RIGHT COOKIE SHEETS

High-quality cookie sheets and baking pans are the second most important secret to perfect cookies. You should use heavy-gauge metal sheets and pans with a dull finish—aluminum is ideal. These double-thick cookie sheets and baking pans will help prevent your cookies from getting overly-dark bottoms. Avoid dark cookie sheets—they can blacken the bottoms of cookies because they absorb more heat. If your cookie sheets are old and discolored, you can line them with foil to help deflect the heat.

Size is important too. Cookie sheets should be at least 2 inches smaller in length and width than your oven so that air can circulate freely around them. So measure your oven before you buy new cookie sheets. If possible, buy flat sheets with only one or two edges turned. They will also help air to circulate around the cookies.

❄

WASH COOKIE SHEETS BY HAND AND PLACE IN OVEN (turned off but still warm from baking) to dry. The same trick works for metal cookie tins; put them upside down in oven.

TIMING IS EVERYTHING

One of the most common mistakes that results in burned or underdone cookies is not timing the baking properly. Fortunately this problem is easily avoided. Buy a good oven thermometer and check it carefully to make sure your oven is at the correct temperature before you start baking. It's also wise to start checking your cookies a couple of minutes before they're supposed to be done. So get a kitchen timer and set it a few minutes early. If you bake two sheets of cookies at once, rotate the cookie sheets between the upper and lower oven racks halfway through baking.

COOL IDEAS

To remove the hot cookie sheets from the oven safely, you will need two sturdy potholders. A cake tester is great for testing bar cookies for doneness. You'll need racks on which to set the baking sheets while the cookies cool. Never set a hot sheet on the counter.

STORING YOUR STASH

Be sure to keep your cookies safe and secure until the day of the cookie swap. Cool cookies completely before packing them so they don't stick together, become misshapen, or get soggy. Tuck treats into self-sealing bags with air squeezed out, metal tins (coffee cans work well), or sturdy plastic containers. Bar cookies can be stored in their baking pan, cut or uncut, covered with a layer of plastic wrap or foil.

Store soft cookies with a wedge of apple or a slice of white bread to keep them moist; replace the fruit or bread every couple of days. Pack soft and crisp cookies separately; otherwise, the crisp ones will absorb moisture from the soft and get soggy. Most cookies will keep at room temperature for 1 to 2 weeks, or freeze for up to 2 to 3 months, or as the recipe directs. To defrost, just unwrap and thaw at room temperature.

IF YOU'RE BAKING YOUR COOKIES FAR IN ADVANCE OF THE SWAP, don't dust them with confectioners' sugar, or glaze or fill them. The sugar will be absorbed, stealing that pretty white finish; the glaze may dry and crystallize; and the jam will harden. For best results, dust, glaze, or fill right before you bring them to the swap.

TIME-SAVING TIPS

Cookie swaps are all about making life easy during the holidays. Here are a few of our favorite test-kitchen tips to make your cookie-baking fast and worry-free.

1 • **Make the dough in advance and freeze it.** Here's a great way to get most of the work out of the way early (what's left—cutting, sprinkling, sampling, inhaling the scent of hot cookies—is pure fun). Just wrap dough in foil, then place in a freezer-weight plastic bag (unless otherwise noted); it should keep in the freezer for up to a month. *Slice-and-bake cookies:* Shape dough into logs or bricks following recipe, then freeze. To bake, slice frozen dough, arrange slices on a cookie sheet, and bake without thawing. *Rolled cookies:* Shape dough into one or more 1-inch-thick disks. Let thaw in the refrigerator overnight before rolling and cutting. *Drop cookies:* Spoon dough into a plastic freezer-safe container. Let thaw in refrigerator 1 to 2 days before baking.

2 • **Set up an assembly line.** Using parchment paper to bake cookies can save time and energy. Unbaked cookies are placed directly

onto the parchment paper, eliminating the need to grease (or wash) the cookie sheet. While a batch of cookies is baking, portion out the remaining cookie dough onto sheets of parchment paper. (If the used parchment has only a few crumbs attached, wipe off and reuse for remaining dough.) When the batch is done baking, simply slide the parchment paper with cooked cookies off the cookie sheet and onto a wire rack (you may need to let the cookies cool slightly before transferring them from the parchment paper directly onto the rack to cool completely.) Then, slide a sheet of parchment paper with raw cookies onto the warm cookie sheet.

3 • **Make bar cookies even easier.** Brownies and other pan cookies are the simplest of all to make, but to speed cleanup and cutting, line pans with foil (extend over edges). When cool, lift edges of foil to remove batch from pan; place on cutting board to cut.

4 • **Bake ahead and freeze your stash.** Cool cookies completely, then wrap and freeze them. *Fragile cookies* (very buttery or crumbly ones): Tuck between layers of waxed paper in airtight freezer containers. *Sturdy cookies* (gingerbread, drop cookies, biscotti): Wrap stacks of four or five in foil or waxed paper, then place in freezer bags. *Decorated cookies:* Freeze in a single layer on a cookie sheet until firm, then pack between layers of waxed paper in airtight freezer containers. *Bar cookies:* Wrap the whole batch, uncut, in foil, or cut into bars and wrap individually in foil or waxed paper, then place in freezer bags. *Note:* Unwrap all cookies before thawing so they don't get soggy from condensation.

HOW THE COOKIE DOESN'T CRUMBLE

Don't let all your hard work crumble while transporting your cookies to and from the swap. Follow these tips for carrying cookies around the corner or shipping them across the country.

If you're bringing them

• Cut and store bar cookies in the pan they were baked in; cover pan with foil or plastic wrap, then arrange cookies on a plate when you get there. (Some 13" by 9" pans come with convenient snap-on plastic lids.)

- For cookies coated with confectioners' sugar, dust them just before you leave, otherwise the sugar will be absorbed and the cookies will lose their sheen.

- If you're transporting decorated sugar cookies or gingerbread cutouts, make sure to arrange them with waxed paper between the layers to protect the pretty designs. The same goes for cookies with sugar glazes or sticky fillings.

If you're shipping them

- Stay away from fragile, buttery cutouts, or you may wind up with Christmas tree stumps and reindeer without antlers. Opt for sturdier varieties, such as drop cookies or bar cookies.

- Use a sturdy cardboard box, plastic storage container, or metal tin lined with impact-absorbing bubble wrap, foam peanuts, popcorn, or crumpled waxed paper.

- Wrap each cookie individually or in pairs back-to-back with plastic wrap or foil, and place in a self-sealing plastic bag for additional protection. If you send crisp cookies, do not pack them with softer ones—they will absorb moisture and get soggy.

- Seal container with tape and place in a heavyweight box; fill in the space around the container with crumpled newspaper or bubble wrap. Clearly mark *fragile* and *perishable*, in big letters, on the outside of the package on all sides.

- Plan ahead. Cookies shipped on a Thursday will sit in a warehouse all weekend, so mail early in the week; packages sent to soldiers overseas must conform to specific military and postal requirements (check usps.com or anysoldier.com for mailing instructions).

- For optimal freshness, consider springing for overnight shipping.

SPECIALTY COOKIE EQUIPMENT

Baking-supply shops have enough cookie-making tools to fill all the shelves in your kitchen, and although it would be fun to have them all, you don't need them. You can bake just about any cookie with just a few additional utensils:

- Cookie cutters of various shapes
- Cookie press for molded cookies
- Cookie scoops
- Grater
- Juicer
- Parchment paper
- Pastry bag and large tips

- Pastry brush
- Pastry cloth
- Pastry wheel
- Rolling pin and pin cover
- Ruler
- Wire whisk
- Yeast thermometer

DECORATING: A SHORT AND SWEET GUIDE

Like cheerfully wrapped packages, cutout cookies with bright trimmings are always inviting. But let's face it, most of us don't have time to pipe on frostings or paint on intricate designs, especially when baking such large batches for a swap. These methods work their magic in minutes and are fun to do with kids.

Before-Baking Brushes

EGG-YOLK WASH. Beat 1 large egg yolk with ¼ teaspoon water. Divide beaten egg among a few small cups and tint each with food coloring.

MILK PAINT. Tint a couple of tablespoons of evaporated milk with food coloring for an old-fashioned glazed look.

After-Baking Flourishes

SUGAR COATING. Boil 1 cup light corn syrup for 1 minute, stirring. Brush syrup on cookie; dust with colored sugar crystals, sprinkles, or candy decors. Or, fill small bowls with trimmings and dip brushed side of cookie into bowl to decorate.

FAST FROSTING. Whisk 1½ cups confectioners' sugar with 1 to 2 tablespoons milk until blended; tint with desired food coloring and brush on.

MARBLING. Brush on an even coat of Ornamental Frosting (opposite). With tip of small paintbrush, drop dots of another frosting color on top. Using a toothpick, drag the edges of the colored dots through the base frosting in a swirling motion to create fanciful designs.

CANDY LAND. Frost cookies with store-bought frosting, then press on chocolate chips, miniature marshmallows, gumdrops, gummy candy, and so on, to create tempting treats.

HOT CHOCOLATE. Melt white or dark chocolate; pour into small self-sealing plastic bag. Snip ⅛ inch off a bottom corner of bag (this is your writing tip). Drizzle over baked cookies. *Variations:* Write names, draw simple shapes such as hearts and stars, or use the chocolate as a glue to anchor decors or candies. Allow 2 hours or more to dry.

ornamental frosting

Use this versatile basic mixture to decorate all your holiday cookies.

MAKES 3 CUPS

1 package (16-ounce) confectioners'
   sugar

3 tablespoons meringue powder (see
   Note)

⅓ cup warm water

Assorted food colorings (optional)

1 • In bowl, with mixer at medium speed, beat confectioners' sugar, meringue powder, and water until blended and mixture is so stiff that knife drawn through it leaves a clean-cut path, about 5 minutes.

2 • If you like, tint frosting with food colorings as desired; keep covered with plastic wrap to prevent drying out.

3 • With small spatula, artists' paintbrushes, or decorating bags with small writing tips, decorate cookies with frosting. (You may need to thin frosting with a little warm water to obtain the right spreading or piping consistency.)

EACH TABLESPOON: 40 calories, 10 g carbohydrate, 3 mg sodium.

NOTE: Meringue powder is available in specialty stores wherever cake-decorating equipment is sold. Or, contact Wilton Industries, 800-794-5866.

THREE STEPS TO ICING COOKIES

Divide Ornamental Frosting (page 25) into bowls. Using food-color pastes, tint each portion of frosting with a different color; cover surfaces with plastic wrap until ready to use, because frosting dries out quickly.

1 • **Apply a base coat.** Using stiff frosting and small writing tip, pipe outline of the area on cookie that you want to fill in; let dry. Place a portion of the frosting into a separate bowl and stir in enough water to thin to the consistency of thick paint. With thinned frosting in decorating bag without tip, or in heavy-duty plastic bag with corner cut to ½-inch opening, squeeze frosting into outlined area. You can also spread frosting with artists' paintbrushes, small metal spatula, or toothpick (depending on size of area) to fill evenly.

2 • **Create a design.** While the frosting on the base is still wet, pipe a series of parallel or curved lines (using stiff frosting in decorating bag outfitted with small writing tip). Then, working quickly, before frosting dries, draw toothpick or tip of knife through lines to make a second set of equally spaced lines perpendicular to the first set. Wipe the toothpick or your knife clean after drawing each line to ensure a neat appearance of the next line. For a different design, alternate directions when drawing toothpick through lines.

3 • **Pipe details.** Use disposable decorating bag or heavy-duty plastic bag, fitted with small writing tip, to pipe stiff Ornamental Frosting for outline or color details (polyester bags will perma-nently discolor). For outlines, hold bag at 45-degree angle with tip almost touching cookie. Squeeze bag with steady, even pressure while piping. Stop squeezing before lifting bag. For dots, hold bag at a 90-degree angle with tip slightly above surface. Squeeze bag without lifting tip, until dot is the desired size. Stop squeezing, then pull bag away.

1

2

3

FIGGY BARS (page 42-43)

BAR COOKIES

FROM BROWNIES AND BLONDIES TO FRUIT-AND-NUT squares, bar cookies are not only delicious but also the easiest of cookies to make. Many of these tempting bars don't even require an electric mixer—you can just stir the batter with a spoon, pat or pour it into a pan, and pop it into the oven.

And because these scrumptious cookies travel well—they can transported right in their baking pan—they're an easy bring-along for your cookie swap.

For great bar cookies every time:

- When baking for a cookie swap, we suggest you avoid any cookies that contain perishable ingredients, such as eggs and cream. Such cookies must be refrigerated and eaten within several days of baking. These would include lemon bars, any cheesecake-type cookies, and any cookies with custard or cream fillings.

- To ensure even baking, rotate cookie sheets or pans between upper and lower oven racks halfway through baking.

- Cool bar cookies completely in the pan before cutting them, then store them in their baking pan, tightly covered with foil or plastic wrap.

- Store cakelike cookies that don't contain perishable ingredients in a tight cookie jar or tin in a cool spot in your kitchen for up to three days. Be sure to add a slice of bread or apple to keep them moist and change it every other day to prevent it from molding.

- To freeze cookies, wrap them tightly first. They will keep well frozen for up to three months, unless otherwise directed.

hermit bars

These spicy fruit bars get their name from their long-keeping quality.

ACTIVE TIME: 20 MINUTES PLUS COOLING • **BAKE TIME:** 26 MINUTES PER BATCH
MAKES 96 COOKIES

———————— ❄ ————————

6 cups all-purpose flour

3 teaspoons ground cinnamon

1½ teaspoons baking powder

1½ teaspoons baking soda

1½ teaspoons ground ginger

¾ teaspoon ground nutmeg

¾ teaspoon salt

½ teaspoon ground cloves

3 cups packed brown sugar

1½ cups butter or margarine
 (3 sticks), softened

1 cup dark molasses

3 large eggs

3 cups dark raisins

3 cups pecans, toasted (see page 15)
 and chopped (optional)

1 • Preheat oven to 350°F. Grease and flour two large cookie sheets.

2 • In large bowl, whisk flour, cinnamon, baking powder, baking soda, ginger, nutmeg, salt, and cloves until blended.

3 • In separate large bowl, with mixer at medium speed, beat brown sugar and butter until light and fluffy. Beat in molasses until well combined. Beat in eggs. Reduce speed to low; beat in flour mixture just until blended, occasionally scraping bowl with rubber spatula. With wooden spoon, stir in raisins and pecans, if using, just until combined.

4 • Divide dough into thirds, then divide each third into quarters. With lightly floured hands, shape each quarter into 12" by 1½" log. Place 2 logs, 3 inches apart, on each prepared cookie sheet. Cover remaining 8 logs with damp kitchen towel.

5 • Bake until logs have flattened and edges are firm, 13 to 15 minutes. Cool logs on cookie sheets on wire racks, about 15 minutes.

6 • Transfer logs to cutting board. Slice each log crosswise into 8 cookies. Transfer cookies to wire racks to cool completely. Grease and flour completely cooled cookie sheets and repeat with remaining 8 logs.

EACH COOKIE: About 105 calories, 1 g protein, 19 g carbohydrate, 3 g total fat (2 g saturated), 15 mg cholesterol, 80 mg sodium.

czechoslovakian cookies

Cookie swaps are great fun any time of year but especially at Christmas. This season, why not go global and bake a big batch of traditional holiday cookies from another country? Kids will love assembling the strawberry and walnut layers of these Eastern European cookies.

ACTIVE TIME: 35 MINUTES • BAKE TIME: 45 MINUTES • MAKES 96 BARS

4 cups butter (8 sticks), softened

4 cups sugar

8 large egg yolks

8 cups all-purpose flour

½ teaspoon salt

4 cups walnuts, chopped

2 cups strawberry preserves

1 • Preheat oven to 350°F. Grease two 15½" by 10" jelly-roll pans.

2 • In large bowl, with mixer at low speed, beat butter and sugar until mixed, occasionally scraping bowl with rubber spatula. Increase speed to high; beat until light and fluffy. Reduce speed to low; beat in egg yolks until well combined, constantly scraping bowl with rubber spatula. Add flour and salt and beat until blended, occasionally scraping bowl. With wooden spoon, stir in chopped walnuts.

3 • With lightly floured hands, divide dough into 4 equal pieces. Pat 1 piece of dough evenly onto bottom of 1 prepared pan. Spread 1 cup strawberry preserves over dough. With lightly floured hands, pinch off ¾-inch pieces from 1 piece of remaining dough and drop over preserves; do not pat down. Repeat with remaining 2 pieces of dough and 1 cup strawberry preserves.

4 • Bake until golden, 45 to 50 minutes. Cool completely in pans on wire racks. When cool, cut each pastry lengthwise into 6 strips, then cut each strip crosswise into 8 pieces.

EACH BAR: About 130 calories, 2 g protein, 11 g carbohydrate, 9 g total fat (4 g saturated), 31 mg cholesterol, 70 mg sodium.

blondies

These golden butterscotch favorites go from saucepan to baking pan in one easy step. For the best taste and texture, carefully follow the instructions for determining doneness. The center should still be slightly moist when the pan is removed from the oven. The blondies will firm up to just the right texture as they cool.

ACTIVE TIME: 10 MINUTES • **BAKE TIME:** 30 MINUTES • **MAKES** 96 BLONDIES

4 cups all-purpose flour

8 teaspoons baking powder

4 teaspoons salt

1½ cups (3 sticks) butter or margarine

7 cups packed light brown sugar

8 teaspoons vanilla extract

8 large eggs

6 cups pecans, coarsely chopped

1 • Preheat oven to 350°F. Grease four 13" by 9" baking pans. In medium bowl, whisk flour, baking powder, and salt until blended.

2 • In 5-quart saucepan, melt butter over low heat. Remove from heat. With wooden spoon, stir in brown sugar and vanilla. Beat in eggs until well blended. Stir in flour mixture just until blended. Stir in pecans. Divide batter equally among prepared pans: spread evenly.

3 • Bake, in two batches, until toothpick inserted 2 inches from edge of pan comes out clean, about 30 minutes. Do not overbake. Blondies will firm as they cool. Cool completely in pans on wire racks.

4 • When cool, cut each pastry lengthwise into 4 strips, then cut each strip crosswise into 6 pieces.

EACH BLONDIE: About 160 calories, 2 g protein, 21 g carbohydrate, 8 g total fat (2 g saturated), 25 mg cholesterol, 180 mg sodium.

praline-topped brownies

Some might think that adding this luscious topping to our rich brownies is a case of gilding the lily—until they taste one.

ACTIVE TIME: 15 MINUTES PLUS COOLING • **BAKE TIME:** 25 MINUTES • **MAKES** 96 BROWNIES

------------------------- ❄ -------------------------

BROWNIES

3¾ cups all-purpose flour

1½ teaspoons salt

2¼ cups butter or margarine (4½ sticks)

12 squares (16 ounces) unsweetened chocolate, chopped

12 squares (16 ounces) semisweet chocolate, chopped

6 cups sugar

3 tablespoons vanilla extract

15 large eggs, beaten

PRALINE TOPPING

15 tablespoons butter

1 cup packed light brown sugar

½ cup bourbon or 4 tablespoons vanilla extract plus 4 tablespoons water

6 cups confectioners' sugar

1½ cups pecans, toasted (see page 15) and coarsely chopped

1 • Preheat oven to 350°F. Grease three 13" by 9" baking pans. In small bowl, whisk flour and salt until blended.

2 • In heavy 4-quart saucepan, melt butter and unsweetened and semisweet chocolates over low heat, stirring frequently, until smooth. Remove from heat. With wooden spoon, stir in sugar and vanilla. Add eggs; stir until well mixed. Stir flour mixture into chocolate mixture just until blended. Divide batter equally among prepared pans; spread evenly.

3 • Bake until toothpick inserted 1 inch from edge comes out clean, 25 to 30 minutes. Cool completely in pans on wire racks.

4 • In 4-quart saucepan, melt butter and brown sugar over medium-low heat until mixture has melted and begins to bubble, about 5 minutes. Remove from heat. With wire whisk, beat in bourbon or vanilla and water. Add confectioners' sugar and stir until smooth.

5 • With small metal spatula, spread one third of topping over room-temperature browniesin each pan; sprinkle evenly with pecans. Cut each pan of brownies lengthwise into 4 strips, then cut each strip crosswise into 8 pieces.

EACH BROWNIE WITH TOPPING: About 297 calories, 3 g protein, 39 g carbohydrate, 15 g total fat (8 g saturated), 66 mg cholesterol, 147 mg sodium.

almond shortbread brownies

This party-size pan of triple-layered chocolate shortbread bars is covered with a layer of rich chocolate ganache. Lining the pan with foil makes it easier to lift them out and cut them without breaking.

ACTIVE TIME: 1 HOUR PLUS COOLING • BAKE TIME: 40 MINUTES • MAKES 96 BROWNIES

————————— ❄ —————————

1 cup whole natural almonds (4 ounces), toasted (see page 15)

¾ cup confectioners' sugar

1¾ cups butter or margarine (3½ sticks), softened

2¾ cups all-purpose flour

¼ teaspoon almond extract

5 squares (5 ounces) unsweetened chocolate, chopped

3 large eggs

2 cups granulated sugar

1¼ teaspoon salt

2 teaspoons vanilla extract

6 squares (6 ounces) semisweet chocolate, chopped

⅓ cup heavy or whipping cream

½ cup sliced almonds, toasted (see page 15)

1 • Preheat oven to 350°F. Line 15½" by 10½" jelly-roll pan with foil, extending foil over rim.

2 • In blender or in food processor with knife blade attached, process whole almonds with ¼ cup confectioners' sugar until nuts are finely ground.

3 • In large bowl, with mixer at low speed, beat ¾ cup butter and remaining ½ cup confectioners' sugar until blended. Increase speed to high and beat mixture until light and fluffy. Reduce speed to low; beat in ground-almond mixture, 1¾ cups flour, and almond extract just until blended (dough will be stiff). With hands, pat dough evenly onto bottom of prepared pan.

4 • Bake until golden, 20 to 25 minutes. Cool in pan on wire rack.

5 • Meanwhile, in heavy 2-quart saucepan, melt unsweetened chocolate and remaining 1 cup butter over low heat, stirring frequently, until smooth. Remove from heat. Cool slightly, about 10 minutes.

6 • In large bowl, with mixer at high speed, beat eggs, granulated sugar, salt, and 1 teaspoon vanilla until ribbon forms when beaters are lifted, 5 to 10 minutes. Beat in cooled chocolate mixture until blended. With wooden spoon, stir in remaining 1 cup flour. Pour chocolate-flour mixture over cooled shortbread crust.

7 • Bake until toothpick inserted 1 inch from edge comes out almost clean, 20 to 25 minutes. Cool in pan on wire rack.

8 • In heavy 2-quart saucepan, melt semisweet chocolate with cream over low heat, stirring frequently until smooth. Remove from heat; stir in remaining 1 teaspoon vanilla.

9 • Remove brownie from pan by lifting edges of foil; transfer to cutting board. Peel foil from sides. With small metal spatula, spread chocolate glaze over brownie. Sprinkle almond slices over top. Let stand at room temperature until set, about 2 hours, or refrigerate 30 minutes. When set, cut lengthwise into 8 strips, then cut each strip crosswise into 12 pieces.

EACH BROWNIE: About 127 calories, 2 g protein, 13 g carbohydrate, 8 g total fat (4 g saturated), 22 mg cholesterol, 57 mg sodium.

lebkuchen

In addition to great texture, these chewy spice bars are loaded with flavor, and they keep so well that you can make them ahead of time.

ACTIVE TIME: 35 MINUTES PLUS COOLING • **BAKE TIME:** 30 MINUTES • **MAKES** 128 COOKIES

❄

2 (16-ounce) boxes dark brown sugar

8 large eggs

3 cups all-purpose flour

3 teaspoons ground cinnamon

2 teaspoons baking powder

1½ teaspoons ground cloves

2 cups walnuts, coarsely chopped

2 cups dark seedless raisins or 1½ cups diced mixed candied fruit

1 cup confectioners' sugar

2 tablespoons fresh lemon juice

1 • Preheat oven to 350°F. Grease two 13" by 9" baking pans. Line both pans with foil, extending foil over rim; grease foil.

2 • In large bowl, with mixer at medium speed, beat brown sugar and eggs until well mixed, about 1 minute, occasionally scraping bowl with rubber spatula. Reduce speed to low; gradually beat in flour, cinnamon, baking powder, and cloves until blended, occasionally scraping bowl. Stir in walnuts and raisins. Spoon equal amount of mixture into each prepared pan and spread evenly.

3 • Bake 30 minutes. Cool completely in pans on wire racks.

4 • In medium bowl, stir confectioners' sugar and lemon juice until smooth. Drizzle icing over Lebkuchen. Let stand until icing has set, about 10 minutes.

5 • Lift Lebkuchen from pans by edges of foil; transfer to cutting board and peel away foil from sides. Cut each pastry lengthwise into 8 strips, then cut each strip crosswise into 8 bars.

EACH BAR: About 65 calories, 1 g protein, 12 g carbohydrate, 2 g total fat (0 g saturated), 13 mg cholesterol, 15 mg sodium.

lemon-cranberry shortbread

Not your grandmother's shortbread, these glazed sweet-tart bars are festive enough for the holidays and pretty enough for afternoon tea or for any occasion when you want something special.

ACTIVE TIME: 30 MINUTES PLUS COOLING • **BAKE TIME:** 35 MINUTES • **MAKES** 96 BARS

4 to 6 lemons

1½ cups cold butter (3 sticks), cut into pieces

½ cup granulated sugar

3 cups confectioners' sugar

4 cups all-purpose flour

1 cup dried cranberries

1 • Preheat oven to 300°F. Line two 13" by 9" baking pans with foil, extending foil over rim.

2 • From lemons, grate 4 tablespoons plus 1 teaspoon peel and squeeze 4 tablespoons plus 2 teaspoons juice.

3 • In food processor with knife blade attached, blend butter, granulated sugar, 1 cup confectioners' sugar, 4 tablespoons lemon peel, and 2 tablespoons lemon juice until creamy. Reserve remaining lemon peel and juice for glaze. Add flour and pulse until dough begins to come together. Add cranberries and pulse until evenly mixed into dough (most cranberries will be chopped, a few will remain whole). Divide dough in half. With hand, press 1 piece of dough evenly onto bottom of each prepared pan.

4 • Bake until edges are lightly browned and top is pale golden, 35 to 40 minutes. Cool completely in pans on wire racks.

5 • In small bowl, with spoon, stir remaining 2 cups confectioners' sugar, 2 tablespoons lemon juice, and 1 teaspoon lemon peel until smooth, adding some of remaining 2 teaspoons juice, if necessary, to obtain good spreading consistency. Spread glaze over both shortbreads. Let stand until glaze sets, about 30 minutes.

6 • Remove shortbreads from pan by lifting edges of foil; transfer to cutting board and peel away foil from sides. Cut each shortbread lengthwise into 4 strips, then cut each strip crosswise into 12 bars.

EACH BAR: About 90 calories, 1 g protein, 13g carbohydrate, 4g total fat (3g saturated), 11 mg cholesterol, 40 mg sodium.

caramel-pecan bars

A tasty trio of pecans, caramel, and chocolate nestled in a sweet, golden pastry crust make these bars a standout in any assortment.

ACTIVE TIME: 1 HOUR PLUS COOLING AND CHILLING • **BAKE TIME:** 25 MINUTES • **MAKES** 96 BARS

COOKIE CRUST

1½ cups butter (3 sticks), softened

1½ cups confectioners' sugar

3 teaspoons vanilla extract

4½ cups all-purpose flour

CARAMEL-PECAN FILLING

2 cups packed brown sugar

1 cup honey

1 cup butter (2 sticks), cut into pieces (do not use margarine)

⅔ cup granulated sugar

½ cup heavy or whipping cream

4 teaspoons vanilla extract

3 cups pecans, toasted (see page 15) and coarsely chopped

4 ounces (4 squares) semisweet chocolate, melted

1 • Preheat oven to 350°F. Grease two 13" by 9" baking pans. Line both pans with foil, extending foil over rim; grease foil.

2 • Prepare crust: In large bowl, with mixer at medium speed, beat butter, confectioners' sugar, and vanilla until creamy, about 2 minutes. Reduce speed to low; gradually beat in flour until evenly moistened (mixture will resemble fine crumbs).

3 • Sprinkle equal amount of crumbs into each prepared pan. With hand, firmly pat crumbs evenly onto bottom of pans.

4 • Bake crusts until lightly browned, 25 to 30 minutes. Cool in pans on wire racks.

5 • Prepare filling: In 3-quart saucepan, heat brown sugar, honey, butter, granulated sugar, cream, and vanilla to full boil over high heat, stirring frequently. Reduce heat to medium-high; set candy thermometer in place and continue cooking, without stirring, until temperature reaches 248°F or firm-ball stage (when small amount of mixture dropped into very cold water forms a firm ball that does not flatten upon removal from water).

6 • Sprinkle pecans evenly over still-warm crust. Pour hot caramel over nuts. Cool in pans on wire racks or until caramel is room temperature and has formed a skin on top, 1 hour.

7 • With fork, drizzle melted chocolate over caramel layer. Cover and refrigerate until cold and chocolate is set, at least 1 hour.

8 • When chocolate is set, lift pastry with foil out of pan and place on cutting board; peel away foil from sides. Cut each pastry lengthwise into 6 strips, then cut each strip crosswise into 8 bars.

EACH BAR: About 140 calories, 1 g protein, 16 g carbohydrate, 8 g total fat (4 g saturated), 15 mg cholesterol, 55 mg sodium.

figgy bars

If these bar cookies remind you of an English steamed pudding, it's no accident; that's exactly the flavor we had in mind—complete with a hard-sauce glaze. But we've slashed the fat by formulating this recipe specifically for trans fat-free vegetable oil spread. (Pictured on page 28.)

ACTIVE TIME: 25 MINUTES PLUS COOLING • **BAKE TIME:** 23 MINUTES PER BATCH
MAKES 96 BARS

FIGGY BARS

10 ounces (scant 2 cups) black mission figs, finely chopped

1 cup water

2 cups quick-cooking oats, uncooked

1½ cups brown sugar

⅔ cup dark molasses

6 tablespoons trans fat–free vegetable oil spread (60% to 70% oil)

2 large eggs

1 cup all-purpose flour

1 cup toasted wheat germ

2 teaspoons pumpkin-pie spice

2 teaspoons freshly grated orange peel

1 teaspoon salt

1 teaspoon baking soda

1 teaspoon baking powder

HARD-SAUCE GLAZE

2 cups confectioners' sugar

¼ cup brandy

2 tablespoons warm water

1 • Preheat oven to 350°F. Lightly spray two 13" by 9" baking pans with nonstick cooking spray. Line both pans with foil, extending foil 2 inches over short sides of pans. Spray foil with cooking spray.

2 • In 4-quart saucepan, combine figs and water; heat to boiling over high heat. Remove saucepan from heat; stir in oats. Stir sugar, molasses, and vegetable oil spread into fig mixture until blended. Stir in eggs. Add flour, wheat germ, pumpkin-pie spice, orange peel, salt, baking soda, and baking powder and stir until combined. Divide batter equally between prepared pans; spread evenly.

3 • Bake until toothpick inserted in center comes out clean, 23 to 26 minutes. Cool in pans on wire racks 10 minutes.

4 • Meanwhile, prepare glaze: In small bowl, stir confectioners' sugar, brandy, and water until blended.

5 • Remove pastry from pans by lifting edges of foil; transfer with foil to racks. Brush both hot pastries with glaze. Cool completely.

6 • When cool, cut each lengthwise into 4 strips, then cut each strip crosswise into 6 rectangles. Cut each rectangle diagonally in half to make 96 triangles. Store in tightly covered container, with waxed paper between layers, at room temperature up to 1 week or in refrigerator up to 1 month.

EACH BAR: About 60 calories, 1 g protein, 12 g carbohydrates, 1 g total fat (0g saturated), 4 mg cholesterol, 50 mg sodium

LINING PAN WITH FOIL: Turn the baking pan bottom side up. Cover the pan tightly with foil, shiny side out. Remove foil cover. Turn the baking pan right side up and carefully fit the molded foil into it, smoothing foil to fit into the edges.

apricot-almond squares

Fruits and nuts are always a popular combination, especially when they come with a sweet pastry crust.

ACTIVE TIME: 30 MINUTES PLUS COOLING • **BAKE TIME:** 1 HOUR 10 MINUTES
MAKES 96 SQUARES

---❄---

APRICOT FILLING

4 cups dried apricots (24 ounces)

1 cup granulated sugar

5 cups water

SWEET PASTRY

4 cups all-purpose flour

1 cup granulated sugar

½ teaspoon salt

1 cup cold butter or margarine (2 sticks), cut into pieces

½ cup vegetable shortening

ALMOND TOPPING

2 tubes or cans (7 to 8 ounces each) almond paste, crumbled

1½ cups granulated sugar

1 cup butter or margarine (2 sticks) softened

6 large eggs

⅔ cup all-purpose flour

2 teaspoons vanilla extract

¼ teaspoon salt

4 tablespoons confectioners' sugar

1 • Prepare filling: In 3-quart saucepan, heat apricots, sugar, and water to boiling over high heat. Reduce heat to medium-low and cook, uncovered, until apricots are very tender, about 20 minutes. Remove saucepan from heat. With potato masher or fork, mash apricots with liquid in saucepan until mixture becomes a thick paste. Cool filling completely.

2 • Meanwhile, prepare pastry: Preheat oven to 350°F. In large bowl, whisk flour, sugar, and salt until blended. With pastry blender or 2 knives used scissor-fashion, cut in butter and shortening until mixture resembles coarse crumbs. Sprinkle 6 to 8 tablespoons ice water, 1 tablespoon at a time, into flour mixture, mixing lightly with fork after each addition, until dough is just moist enough to hold together.

3 • Divide dough in half. Press 1 piece of dough evenly onto bottom of ungreased 15½" by 10½" jelly-roll pan. Repeat with remaining dough and separate pan.

4 • Bake pastries until golden brown, 25 to 30 minutes. Cool completely in pans on wire racks.

5 • Meanwhile, prepare topping: In food processor with knife blade attached, pulse almond paste, sugar, and butter until mixture is crumbly. Add eggs and pulse until smooth, scraping bowl with rubber spatula if necessary. Add flour, vanilla, and salt, and pulse just until combined. Spread equal amount of cooled filling evenly over each baked pastry. Pour equal amount of topping evenly over filling.

6 • Bake until tops are golden, 40 to 45 minutes. Cool completely in pans on wire racks.

7 • Sprinkle top of both apricot squares with confectioners' sugar. Cut each lengthwise into 6 strips, then cut each strip crosswise into 8 squares.

EACH SQUARE: About 125 calories, 2 g protein, 17 g carbohydrate, 6 g total fat (3 g saturated), 22 mg cholesterol, 60 mg sodium.

OATMEAL COOKIES (page 49)

DROP COOKIES

QUICK TO MIX UP, FUN TO SPOON ONTO COOKIE SHEETS, and easy to bake, drop cookies offer almost immediate gratification. They're perfect cookie-swap contenders—especially if little hands want to join in the fun.

Although drop cookies are a snap to make, follow these tips so they come out perfect.

- To promote even baking, make sure each ball of raw cookie dough is the same size.

- You can use a measuring spoon to scoop up equal portions of dough for each cookie or invest in a cookie scoop that will measure the dough as well as push it out onto the sheet.

- For perfectly shaped cookies, leave enough space between the drops of dough so that the cookies don't spread together during baking. Unless the recipe directs otherwise, 2 inches apart is a good standard.

- To ensure even baking, rotate cookie sheets or pans between upper and lower oven racks halfway through baking.

- To prevent the dough from spreading, cool the sheets between batches. Spreading dough causes the cookies to run together and creates a very thin cookie that is more likely to burn. Simply run lukewarm water first and then cool water over the back of the sheets between each batch.

- To prevent cookies from sticking to the sheets, always check greased sheets to see if they need regreasing between batches.

chewy chocolate-cherry oatmeal cookies

We like the luxury of chocolate chips and tart dried cherries, but if you're wedded to tradition, feel free to use just raisins. For chewy cookies, bake the minimum time; for crispy, bake a few minutes longer.

ACTIVE TIME: 45 MINUTES PLUS COOLING • **BAKE TIME:** 12 MINUTES PER BATCH
MAKES ABOUT 108 COOKIES

3 cups all-purpose flour

4 teaspoons baking soda

1 teaspoon salt

1½ cups granulated sugar

1½ cups packed brown sugar

1½ cups butter or margarine
(3 sticks), softened

4 large eggs

4 teaspoons vanilla extract

6 cups old-fashioned oats,
uncooked

2 cups dried tart cherries or raisins

2 packages (6 ounces each) semi
sweet chocolate chips (2 cups)

1 • Preheat oven to 350°F. Grease two large cookie sheets. In small bowl, with wire whisk, stir flour, baking soda, and salt until blended.

2 • In large bowl, with mixer at medium speed, beat granulated and brown sugars and butter until creamy, occasionally scraping bowl with rubber spatula. Beat in eggs, one at a time, beating well after each addition. Beat in vanilla. Reduce speed to low; gradually beat in flour mixture just until blended, occasionally scraping bowl. With wooden spoon, stir in oats, dried cherries, and chocolate chips.

3 • Drop dough by rounded measuring tablespoons, 2 inches apart, onto prepared cookie sheets.

4 • Bake cookies until tops are golden, 12 to 14 minutes. With wide spatula, transfer cookies to wire racks to cool. Repeat with remaining dough.

EACH COOKIE: About 100 calories, 1 g protein, 15 g carbohydrate, 4 g total fat (2 g saturated), 15 mg cholesterol, 100 mg sodium.

peanut butter cookies

These classic cookies are a must for any cookie swap. If you like, instead of crosshatching the cookies with a fork, lightly press mini non-melting chocolate-covered candies into the top of each cookie before baking.

ACTIVE TIME: 45 MINUTES • **BAKE TIME:** 12 MINUTES PER BATCH • **MAKES** ABOUT 144 COOKIES

4 cups all-purpose flour

2 teaspoons baking powder

3 teaspoons baking soda

1½ teaspoons salt

2 jars (18 ounces each) creamy peanut butter

2 cups butter (4 sticks), softened

2 cups packed brown sugar

2 cups (plus ¼ cup) granulated sugar

4 large eggs

2 teaspoons vanilla extract

1 • Preheat oven to 350°F. In medium bowl, with wire whisk, stir flour, baking powder, baking soda, and salt until blended.

2 • In large bowl, with mixer at medium speed, beat peanut butter, butter, brown and 2 cups granulated sugars until creamy, occasionally scraping bowl with rubber spatula. Reduce speed to low; beat in vanilla, then eggs, one at a time, beating well after each addition. Add peanut butter and beat on medium speed 2 minutes or until creamy. Reduce speed to low. Beat in flour mixture just until blended, occasionally scraping bowl.

3 • Drop dough by rounded measuring tablespoons, 2 inches apart, onto two ungreased large cookie sheets. Place remaining granulated sugar on plate. Dip times of fork in sugar, then press crisscross pattern into top of each cookie.

4 • Bake until lightly browned, 12 to 14 minutes. With wide spatula, transfer cookies to wire racks to cool completely. Repeat with remaining dough and sugar.

EACH COOKIE: About 100 calories, 3 g protein, 9 g carbohydrate, 6 g total fat (2 g saturated), 13 mg cholesterol, 114 mg sodium.

MAKING CRISSCROSS PATTERN: Whether you drop the dough or shape it into balls, flattening the peanut butter dough with a fork give it its classic finish.

drop sugar cookies

If you don't have the time to make roll-and-cut sugar cookies, try this simple recipe. For variety, stir in ½ cup chopped nuts, ½ cup mini chocolate chips, or 1 tablespoon freshly grated lemon peel. You can also decorate the cookies with piped icing after baking.

ACTIVE TIME: 35 MINUTES • **BAKE TIME:** 14 MINUTES PER BATCH • **MAKES** ABOUT 126 COOKIES

6 cups all-purpose flour

3 teaspoons baking powder

¾ teaspoon salt

2¼ cups butter or margarine (4½ sticks), softened

3 cups sugar

3 eggs

9 tablespoons milk

6 tablespoons vanilla extract

1 • Preheat oven to 350°F. In medium bowl, whisk flour, baking powder, and salt until blended.

2 • In large bowl, with mixer at medium-low speed, beat butter and sugar until creamy. Add eggs, milk, and vanilla; beat until well blended. Reduce speed to low; beat in flour mixture just until blended.

3 • Drop dough by rounded measuring tablespoons, 2 inches apart, onto two ungreased large cookie sheets.

4 • Bake until edges are browned, about 14 minutes. With wide spatula, transfer cookies to wire rack to cool completely. Repeat with remaining cookie dough.

EACH COOKIE: About 70 calories, 1 g protein, 9 g carbohydrate, 3 g total fat (2 g saturated), 14 mg cholesterol, 60 mg sodium.

coconut macaroons

A traditional Passover sweet, these flourless cookies are delicious any time of the year. They're also a welcome treat to people who are allergic to wheat or gluten.

ACTIVE TIME: 20 MINUTES • **BAKE TIME:** 25 MINUTES PER BATCH • **MAKES** ABOUT 126 COOKIES

9 cups flaked sweetened coconut

2¼ cups sugar

12 large egg whites

¾ teaspoon salt

3 teaspoons vanilla extract

½ teaspoon almond extract

1 • Preheat oven to 325°F. Line two cookie sheets with parchment or foil.

2 • In large bowl, stir coconut, sugar, egg whites, salt, vanilla, and almond extract until well combined.

3 • Drop dough by rounded measuring teaspoons, 1 inch apart, onto prepared cookie sheets.

4 • Bake until cookies are set and lightly golden, about 25 minutes. Cool 1 minute on cookie sheets. With wide metal spatula, transfer cookies to wire racks to cool completely. Repeat with remaining dough.

EACH COOKIE: About 41 calories, 1 g protein, 6 g carbohydrate, 2 g total fat (2 g saturated), 0 mg cholesterol, 32 mg sodium.

double chocolate-cherry drops

This combination of dried tart cherries and a double dose of rich chocolate from semisweet chunks and cocoa is a cookie lover's dream.

ACTIVE TIME: 35 MINUTES PLUS COOLING • **BAKE TIME:** 10 MINUTES PER BATCH
MAKES ABOUT 120 COOKIES

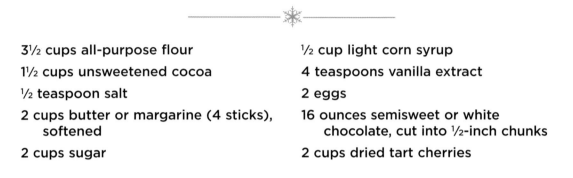

3½ cups all-purpose flour

1½ cups unsweetened cocoa

½ teaspoon salt

2 cups butter or margarine (4 sticks), softened

2 cups sugar

½ cup light corn syrup

4 teaspoons vanilla extract

2 eggs

16 ounces semisweet or white chocolate, cut into ½-inch chunks

2 cups dried tart cherries

1 • Preheat oven to 350°F. In medium bowl, whisk together flour, cocoa, and salt until blended.

2 • In large bowl, with mixer at medium speed, beat butter and sugar until creamy, occasionally scraping bowl with rubber spatula. Beat in corn syrup, vanilla, and eggs until well mixed. Reduce speed to low. Gradually add flour mixture; beat just until blended, occasionally scraping bowl. With wooden spoon, stir in chocolate chunks and cherries.

3 • Drop cookies by rounded measuring teaspoons, 2 inches apart, onto two ungreased large cookie sheets.

4 • Bake until tops are just firm, 10 to 11 minutes. Transfer cookies to wire racks to cool. Repeat with remaining dough.

EACH COOKIE: About 85 calories, 1 g protein, 11 g carbohydrate, 5 g total fat (3 g saturated), 12 mg cholesterol, 50 mg sodium.

hazelnut cookies

These melt-in-the-mouth hazelnut meringues are a double treat, sandwiched together and decorated with melted chocolate. Because they are made in a low oven, the cookies are actually dried rather than baked.

ACTIVE TIME: 1 HOUR PLUS COOLING • **BAKE TIME:** 25 MINUTES • **MAKES** ABOUT 96 COOKIES

4 cups hazelnuts (filberts), toasted (see page 15)

1½ cups sugar

10 large egg whites

⅔ cups all-purpose flour

10 tablespoons butter or margarine, melted and cooled

12 squares (12 ounces) semisweet chocolate, melted and cooled

1 • Preheat oven to 275°F. Grease two large cookie sheets. In food processor with knife blade attached, process hazelnuts and ½ cup sugar until nuts are finely ground.

2 • In large bowl, with mixer at high speed, beat egg whites until soft peaks form when beaters are lifted. Increase speed to high and sprinkle in remaining 1 cup sugar, 1 tablespoon at a time, beating well after each addition, until sugar has completely dissolved and whites stand in stiff peaks. With rubber spatula, fold in ground hazelnuts, flour, and melted butter.

3 • Drop mixture by rounded measuring teaspoons, about 2 inches apart, on prepared cookie sheets.

4 • Bake until cookies are firm and edges are golden, 25 minutes. With wide metal spatula, transfer cookies to wire racks to cool. Repeat with remaining batter.

5 • When cookies are cool, with small metal spatula, spread flat side of half the cookies with thin layer of melted chocolate. Top with remaining cookies, flat side down, to make sandwiches. Spoon remaining chocolate into small zip-tight plastic bag; snip 1 corner of bag to make small hole. Squeeze thin lines of chocolate over cookies. Let stand until set.

EACH SANDWICH COOKIE: About 75 calories, 1 g protein, 7 g carbohydrate, 5 g total fat (0 g saturated), 0 mg cholesterol, 25 mg sodium.

christmas fruit drops

Chewy and colorful with candied red and green cherries, crunchy with toasted walnuts and rice cereal, and rich, with white chocolate chips, these cookies are practically a celebration unto themselves.

ACTIVE TIME: 35 MINUTES PLUS COOLING • **BAKE TIME:** 10 MINUTES PER BATCH
MAKES ABOUT 144 COOKIES

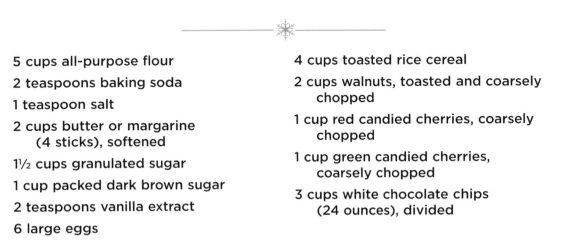

5 cups all-purpose flour

2 teaspoons baking soda

1 teaspoon salt

2 cups butter or margarine (4 sticks), softened

1½ cups granulated sugar

1 cup packed dark brown sugar

2 teaspoons vanilla extract

6 large eggs

4 cups toasted rice cereal

2 cups walnuts, toasted and coarsely chopped

1 cup red candied cherries, coarsely chopped

1 cup green candied cherries, coarsely chopped

3 cups white chocolate chips (24 ounces), divided

1 • Preheat oven to 350°F. Grease two large cookie sheets.

2 • In medium bowl, whisk flour, baking soda, and salt until blended. In large bowl, with mixer at medium speed, beat butter and granulated and brown sugars until creamy, occasionally scraping bowl with rubber spatula. Beat in vanilla. Add eggs, one at a time, beating well after each addition. Reduce speed to low. Gradually add flour mixture; beat just until blended, occasionally scraping bowl. With spoon, stir in cereal, walnuts, cherries, and 2 cups white chocolate chips.

3 • Drop dough by rounded measuring teaspoons, 1 inch apart, onto prepared cookie sheets.

4 • Bake cookies until golden, 10 to 11 minutes. Transfer cookies to wire rack to cool. Repeat with remaining dough.

5 • In small microwave-safe bowl, melt remaining 1 cup white chocolate chips in microwave on Medium (50% power), stirring once, until smooth, about 2 minutes. Place cookies on waxed paper; drizzle with melted chocolate. Let stand until chocolate has set.

EACH COOKIE: About 100 calories, 1 g protein, 12 g carbohydrates, 6 g total fat, (2 g saturated), 17 mg cholesterol, 80 mg sodium.

florentines

A pastry-shop favorite, elegant Florentines are easy to make at home. The only tricky part is knowing when to remove them from the cookie sheet, as they are very sticky. If you do it too soon, the cookies are too soft; if you wait until they're completely cool, they'll stick. So let them cool slightly, just until you can handle them, then transfer them to a rack. Florentines travel very well: Just sandwich two with the chocolate as a filling in the middle.

ACTIVE TIME: 40 MINUTES PLUS COOLING • **BAKE TIME:** 10 MINUTES PER BATCH
MAKES ABOUT 96 COOKIES

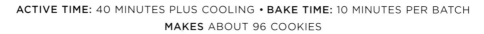

¾ cup butter (1½ sticks),
   cut into pieces

½ cup heavy or whipping cream

2 tablespoons light corn syrup

1 cup sugar

¼ cup all-purpose flour

2 cups slivered almonds,
   finely chopped

1 cup candied orange peel,
   finely chopped

16 squares (16 ounces) semisweet
   chocolate, melted

1 • Preheat oven to 350°F. Line two large cookie sheets with parchment.

2 • In 1-quart saucepan, melt butter with cream, corn syrup, sugar, and flour, stirring frequently. Remove saucepan from heat; stir in almonds and candied orange peel.

3 • Drop batter by rounded measuring teaspoons, 2 inches apart, on prepared cookie sheets. (Do not place more than six cookies on a sheet.)

4 • Bake just until set, about 10 minutes. Cool on cookie sheets on wire racks 1 minute. With wide metal spatula, transfer cookies to wire racks to cool. If cookies become too hard to remove, return sheet to oven briefly to soften. Repeat with remaining batter.

5 • With small metal spatula or butter knife, spread flat side of each cookie with melted chocolate. Return to wire racks, chocolate side up, and let stand until chocolate has set.

EACH COOKIE: About 70 calories, 1 g protein, 8 g carbohydrate, 5 g total fat (2 g saturated), 6 mg cholesterol, 15mg sodium.

From center left: Walnut Horns (page 81),
Noisettines (page 101), and Finska Kakor (page 80).

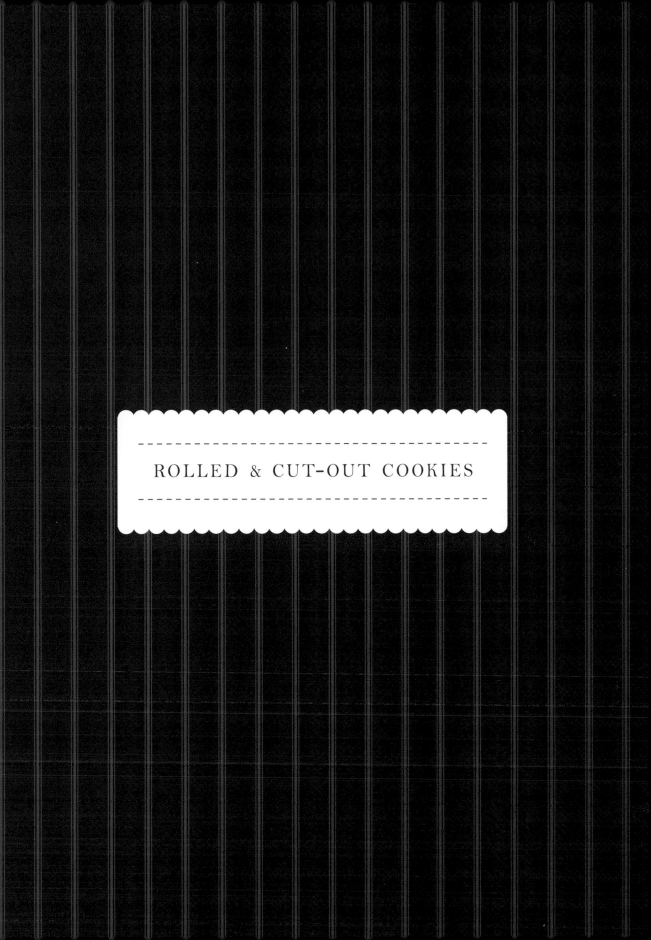

ROLLED & CUT-OUT COOKIES

HERE ARE THE COOKIES DREAMS ARE MADE OF. ROLLED cookies might require a bit more time and effort to prepare, but the pretty cutouts or traditional roll-ups that result are a gift of love, works of art to be appreciated visually before savoring.

That doesn't mean they're too much trouble for a cookie swap. They are great make-aheads. You can prepare several batches at once and keep the dough in the freezer for up to three months, ready to roll out and bake. For even quicker prepping and less cleanup, you can roll out the dough between sheets of waxed paper and tightly wrap it in plastic wrap before freezing. Then, when you're ready to bake, all you have to do is cut the sheets of dough into shapes.

Here are some tips that will make it easy.

- Chill the dough thoroughly before rolling. For convenience, you might want to make the dough a day ahead and refrigerate overnight.

- For easier rolling, dust the work surface lightly and evenly with flour before you roll out the dough. Also rub the rolling pin with flour to keep it from sticking to the dough.

- If chilled dough cracks when rolled, let it stand at room temperature to soften slightly, then try again.

- Cut out cookies as close together as possible so that you have less dough to reroll. Cookies made from the rerolled dough may be tough.

- To ensure even baking, rotate cookie sheets or pans between upper and lower oven racks halfway through baking.

classic sugar cookies

Here's the perfect, all-purpose sugar-cookie dough. You can slice it into diamonds with a knife and sprinkle with colored sugar or cut it into shapes with cookie cutters and decorate with frosting.

ACTIVE TIME: 1 HOUR 30 MINUTES PLUS CHILLING • **BAKE TIME:** 12 MINUTES PER BATCH
MAKES ABOUT 152 COOKIES

6 cups all-purpose flour

1 teaspoon baking powder

1 teaspoon salt

2 cups butter (4 sticks), softened

3 cups sugar

4 large eggs

2 teaspoons vanilla extract

1 • In large bowl, whisk flour, baking powder, and salt until blended. In separate large bowl, with mixer at low speed, beat butter and sugar until blended. Increase speed to high; beat until light and fluffy, about 5 minutes. Reduce speed to low; beat in eggs and vanilla until mixed, then beat in flour mixture just until blended, occasionally scraping bowl with rubber spatula.

2 • Divide dough in half, then divide each half into 4 equal pieces; flatten each into a disk. Wrap each disk in plastic wrap and refrigerate overnight.

3 • Preheat oven to 350°F. On lightly floured surface, with floured rolling pin, roll 1 piece of dough until slightly less than ¼ inch thick; keep remaining dough refrigerated. With floured 3- to 4-inch cookie cutters, cut dough into as many cookies as possible; reserve trimmings. Place cookies, 1 inch apart, on two ungreased large cookie sheets.

4 • Bake until edges are golden, 12 to 15 minutes. With wide metal spatula, transfer cookies to wire racks to cool completely. Repeat with remaining dough and trimmings.

EACH COOKIE: About 61 calories, 1 g protein, 8 g carbohydrate, 3 g total fat (2 g saturated), 13 mg cholesterol, 47 mg sodium.

cinnamon spirals

Butter-and-cream cheese rich, these spirals cookies
taste even better than they look.

ACTIVE TIME: 40 MINUTES PLUS CHILLING • **BAKE:** 12 MINUTES • **MAKES** ABOUT 120 COOKIES

1 cup butter or margarine
    (2 sticks), softened

8 ounces cream cheese, softened

2½ cups all-purpose flour

½ teaspoon salt

⅔ cup sugar

2 teaspoons ground cinnamon

1 • In large bowl, with mixer at medium speed, beat butter and cream cheese until creamy, about 2 minutes. Reduce speed to low; gradually beat in flour and salt until well mixed, occasionally scraping bowl with rubber spatula.

2 • Divide dough in half. On sheet of plastic wrap, pat 1 piece of dough into small rectangle; wrap tightly and refrigerate 1 hour or until dough is firm enough to roll. (Or freeze dough for 30 minutes.) Repeat with remaining dough.

3 • Meanwhile, in small bowl, stir sugar and cinnamon until blended.

4 • On lightly floured surface, with floured rolling pin, roll 1 piece of dough into 15" by 12" rectangle. Sprinkle half of cinnamon-sugar mixture evenly over dough. Starting from a long side, tightly roll rectangle jelly-roll fashion. Brush last ½ inch of dough with water to seal edge. Cut log crosswise in half. Slide logs onto ungreased cookie sheet; cover with plastic wrap and refrigerate 2 hours or until dough is firm enough to slice. (Or freeze dough for 45 minutes.) Repeat with remaining dough and cinnamon-sugar mixture.

5 • Preheat oven to 400° F. Remove 2 logs from freezer; with serrated knife, cut each log crosswise into ¼-inch-thick slices. Place cookies, ½ inch apart, on two ungreased large cookie sheets.

6 • Bake cookies until lightly browned, 12 to 14 minutes. Transfer cookies to wire rack to cool. Repeat with remaining 2 logs.

EACH COOKIE: 45 calories, 1 g protein, 4 g carbohydrate, 3 g total fat (2 g saturated), 8 mg cholesterol, 40 mg sodium

nutmeg bells

Great to decorate for the holidays, but you don't need a formal celebration to enjoy this flavorful take on sugar cookies.

ACTIVE TIME: 1 HOUR PLUS CHILLING, COOLING, AND DECORATING
BAKE TIME: 10 MINUTES PER BATCH • **MAKES** ABOUT 130 COOKIES

---

2 cups butter (4 sticks), softened

2 cups sugar

4 large eggs

4 teaspoons vanilla extract

7 cups all-purpose flour

8 teaspoons baking powder

2 teaspoons salt

2 teaspoons ground nutmeg

Ornamental Frosting
(optional, see page 25)

1 • In large bowl, with mixer at medium speed, beat butter and sugar until creamy, about 3 minutes. Reduce speed to low; beat in eggs and vanilla until blended. Gradually beat in flour, baking powder, salt, and nutmeg until well blended, occasionally scraping bowl with rubber spatula.

2 • Divide dough into 6 equal pieces; flatten each piece into a disk. Wrap each disk in plastic wrap and refrigerate until dough is firm enough to roll, at least 2 hours.

3 • Preheat oven to 325°F. On lightly floured surface, with floured rolling pin, roll 1 piece of dough ⅛ inch thick. With floured 3½-inch bell-shaped cookie cutter, cut dough into as many cookies as possible; wrap and refrigerate trimmings. Place cookies, 1 inch apart, on ungreased large cookie sheets.

4 • Bake until lightly browned, 10 to 12 minutes. With wide metal spatula, transfer cookies to wire rack to cool. Repeat with remaining dough and trimmings.

5 • When cookies are cool, prepare Ornamental Frosting, if using, to decorate cookies; let dry completely, about 1 hour.

EACH COOKIE WITHOUT FROSTING: About 75 calories, 1 g protein, 11 g carbohydrate, 3 g total fat (2 g saturated), 14 mg cholesterol, 90 mg sodium.

sour cream–sugar cookies

The silken texture and melt-in-your-mouth goodness of these cookies come from sour cream.

ACTIVE TIME: 35 MINUTES PLUS CHILLING • **BAKE TIME:** 8 MINUTES PER BATCH
MAKES ABOUT 155 COOKIES

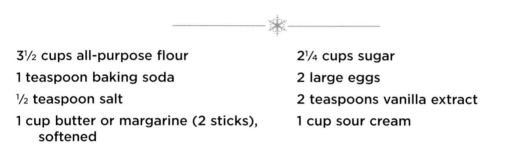

3½ cups all-purpose flour

1 teaspoon baking soda

½ teaspoon salt

1 cup butter or margarine (2 sticks), softened

2¼ cups sugar

2 large eggs

2 teaspoons vanilla extract

1 cup sour cream

1 • In large bowl, whisk flour, baking soda, and salt until blended.

2 • In separate large bowl, with mixer at medium speed, beat butter and 2 cups sugar until combined. Reduce speed to low; beat in egg and vanilla until blended. Beat in sour cream. Beat in flour mixture until combined, scraping bowl occasionally with rubber spatula.

3 • Divide dough in half, then shape each half into 4 balls; flatten balls slightly. Wrap each ball in waxed paper and refrigerate at least 2 hours, or overnight, until dough is firm enough to roll. (If using margarine, refrigerate overnight.)

4 • Preheat oven to 325°F. On lightly floured surface, with floured rolling pin, roll 1 piece of dough ⅛ inch thick. Keep remaining dough refrigerated. With floured 2-inch cookie cutters, cut as many cookies as possible; reserve trimmings. Place cookies, about ½ inch apart, on ungreased large cookie sheets. Sprinkle with some of remaining ¼ cup sugar.

5 • Bake 8 minutes. With wide spatula, transfer cookies to wire racks to cool completely. Repeat with remaining dough, trimmings, and sugar.

EACH COOKIE: About 35 calories, 0 g protein, 5 g carbohydrate, 2 g total fat (1 g saturated), 7 mg cholesterol, 30 mg sodium.

shortbread bites

These shortbread morsels are small, but packed with buttery richness.
You won't be able to stop at just one—and neither will anyone else.

ACTIVE TIME: 30 MINUTES PLUS COOLING • **BAKE TIME:** 18 MINUTES PER BATCH
MAKES 320 COOKIES

2½ **cups all-purpose flour**

6 **tablespoons sugar**

1 **cup (2 sticks) cold butter, cut into pieces**

2 **tablespoons red and green non pareils or sprinkles or 1 cup mini baking bits**

1 • Preheat oven to 325°F.

2 • In food processor with knife blade attached, pulse flour and sugar until combined. Add butter and pulse until dough begins to come together. Place dough in medium bowl. With hand, gently knead in nonpareils or baking bits until evenly blended and dough forms a ball.

3 • Divide dough in half. On lightly floured waxed paper, pat each piece of dough into 8" by 5" rectangle; freeze 15 minutes. Remove first rectangle of dough from freezer and cut into ½-inch squares. Place squares, ½ inch apart, on ungreased large cookie sheets. Repeat with remaining dough rectangles.

4 • Bake cookies until lightly browned on bottom, 18 to 20 minutes, rotating pans between upper and lower racks halfway through baking. Transfer cookies to wire rack to cool.

EACH 4 COOKIES: About 40 calories, 0 g protein, 4 g carbohydrate 3 g total fat (2 g saturated), 7 mg cholesterol, 25 mg sodium

lemon hearts

These delicate holiday sweets are equally at home at cookie swaps or afternoon tea.

ACTIVE TIME: 40 MINUTES PLUS COOLING • **BAKE TIME:** ABOUT 15 MINUTES PER BATCH
MAKES ABOUT 144 COOKIES

LEMON COOKIES

6 cups all-purpose flour

6 tablespoons cornstarch

1½ teaspoons salt

3 cups (6 sticks) butter

2 cups confectioners' sugar

2 tablespoons freshly grated
    lemon peel

3 teaspoons lemon extract

½ teaspoon almond extract

LEMON GLAZE

3 cups confectioners' sugar

3 tablespoons fresh lemon juice

3 teaspoons freshly grated
    lemon peel

1 • Prepare cookies: Preheat oven to 325°F. In large bowl, wisk flour, corn-starch, and salt until blended.

2 • In separate large bowl, with mixer at medium speed, beat butter and sugar until creamy, occasionally scraping bowl with rubber spatula. Beat in lemon peel and extracts. Reduce speed to low; gradually beat in flour mixture until blended, occasionally scraping bowl.

3 • Divide dough into 4 equal pieces. Between two 20-inch sheets of waxed paper, roll 1 piece of dough ⅜ inch thick. (If paper wrinkles during rolling, peel it off and replace it to remove wrinkles.) With floured 2¼-inch heart-shaped cookie cutter, cut dough into as many cookies as possible. With floured ¾-inch heart-shaped cookie cutter, cut out and remove centers from cookies. Reserve centers and trimmings to reroll. With lightly floured wide spatula, carefully place cookies, 1 inch apart, on ungreased large cookie sheets. (If dough becomes too soft to transfer to cookie sheet, freeze 10 minutes until firm.)

4 • Bake cookies until edges are golden, 15 to 16 minutes. Transfer cookies to wire rack; cool 10 minutes.

5 • Meanwhile, prepare lemon glaze: In small bowl, with wire whisk or fork, mix confectioners' sugar, lemon juice, and lemon peel until blended. Dip top side of each warm cookie into glaze. Place cookies on wire rack set over waxed paper to catch any drips. Allow glaze to set, about 20 minutes.

6 • Repeat with remaining dough, reserved centers, trimmings, and glaze, adding a little water to glaze if it begins to thicken.

EACH COOKIE: About 75 calories, 1 g protein, 9 g carbohydrate, 4 g total fat (3 g saturated), 11 mg cholesterol, 65 mg sodium

brown-sugar holly leaves

These cookies translate deliciously into any shape and are great for decorating. They're easy enough for a rainy-day family activity.

ACTIVE TIME: 1 HOUR 30 MINUTES PLUS CHILLING AND COOLING
BAKE TIME: 10 MINUTES PER BATCH • **MAKES** ABOUT 108 COOKIES

———————— ❄ ————————

2 cups butter (4 sticks), cut into pieces

7 cups all-purpose flour

1½ teaspoons baking soda

¾ teaspoon salt

2¼ cups packed brown sugar

¾ cup granulated sugar

3 large eggs

3 teaspoons vanilla extract

Green sugar crystals and cinnamon red-hot candies (optional)

1 • In 2-quart saucepan, heat butter over medium heat until melted and lightly browned. Pour browned butter into small bowl and refrigerate until cold but not firm, about 1 hour 30 minutes.

2 • Meanwhile, in large bowl, whisk flour, baking soda, and salt until blended.

3 • In separate large bowl, with mixer at medium speed, beat browned butter, brown sugar, and granulated sugar until creamy, occasionally scraping bowl with rubber spatula. Add eggs and vanilla and beat until well mixed. Reduce speed to low; gradually beat in flour mixture until blended. (Dough will be crumbly; gather together with hand to form a ball.)

4 • Divide dough into thirds, then divide each third into 3 equal pieces. Between two 12-inch sheets of waxed paper, roll 1 piece of dough ⅛ inch thick. (If paper wrinkles during rolling, peel it off and replace it to remove wrinkles.) Repeat with each piece of remaining dough. Refrigerate dough until firm enough to cut, about 2 hours. Or, place dough in freezer 30 minutes.

5 • Preheat oven to 350°F. Working with 1 piece of dough at a time, peel off top sheet of waxed paper and replace. Turn dough over and remove top sheet of waxed paper. With 3-inch holly leaf–shaped cookie cutter, cut out as many cookies as possible, reserving trimmings. (If dough is too firm and cracks, let stand 5 minutes to soften slightly.) Place cookies, 1 inch apart, on ungreased large cookie sheets. Wrap and refrigerate trimmings.

6 • Using back of paring knife, draw lines on cookies to resemble veins. Sprinkle green sugar along lines and press some cinnamon candies at one end to resemble holly berries, if you like.

7 • Bake cookies until edges are lightly browned, 10 to 12 minutes. Transfer cookies to wire racks to cool. Repeat with remaining dough and trimmings.

EACH COOKIE WITHOUT DECORATION: About 110 calories, 1 g protein, 1 g carbohydrate, 6 g total fat (3 g saturated), 21 mg cholesterol, 95 mg sodium.

apricot–raspberry rugelach

There are many varieties of these Eastern European specialty, but rugelach are always made with cream cheese, filled with fruit and nuts, and have the characteristic rolled crescent shape.

ACTIVE TIME: 1 HOUR PLUS CHILLING • BAKE TIME: 35 MINUTES PER BATCH
MAKES 96 RUGELACH

2 cups butter or margarine (4 sticks), softened

2 packages (8 ounces each) cream cheese, softened

1½ cups granulated sugar

2 teaspoons vanilla extract

½ teaspoon salt

4 cups all-purpose flour

2 cups walnuts (8 ounces), chopped

1½ cups dried apricots, chopped

½ cup packed light brown sugar

3 teaspoons ground cinnamon

1 cup seedless raspberry preserves

2 tablespoons milk

1 • In large bowl, with mixer at low speed, beat butter and cream cheese until creamy. Beat in ½ cup granulated sugar, vanilla, and salt, then beat in 2 cups flour. With wooden spoon, stir in remaining 2 cups flour just until blended.

2 • Divide dough in half, then divide each half into 4 equal pieces; flatten each into a disk. Wrap each disk in waxed paper and refrigerate until firm, at least 2 hours.

3 • In medium bowl, stir walnuts, apricots, brown sugar, ¾ granulated sugar, and 1 teaspoon cinnamon until well mixed. Line two large cookie sheets with foil; grease foil.

4 • On lightly floured surface, with floured rolling pin, roll 1 disk of dough into 9-inch round; keep remaining dough refrigerated. Spread 2 tablespoons preserves over dough. Sprinkle with ½ cup walnut mixture; gently press to adhere. With pastry wheel or sharp knife, cut dough into 12 equal wedges. Starting at curved edge, roll up each wedge, jelly-roll fashion. Place cookies, point side down, ½ inch apart, on prepared cookie sheets; shape into crescents.

5 • Preheat oven to 325°F. In cup, stir remaining ¼ cup granulated sugar and remaining 1 teaspoon cinnamon until blended. With pastry brush, brush rugelach with milk. Sprinkle evenly with some cinnamon-sugar.

6 • Bake until golden, 35 to 40 minutes. With wide metal spatula, immediately transfer rugelach to wire racks to cool completely. Repeat with remaining dough, 1 disk at a time.

EACH RUGELACH: About 116 calories, 1 g protein, 12 g carbohydrate, 7 g total fat (4 g saturated), 16 mg cholesterol, 67 mg sodium.

CUTTING AND SHAPING RUGELACH: After spreading the filling on rugelach dough, cut into wedges using a pastry wheel or a sharp knife.

Starting from wide end, roll up rugelach wedges. Place with the point down and shape into a crescent.

holiday stained-glass cookies

We like to use this easy-to-handle sugar cookie dough for any holiday cut-out cookies—especially this one. The crushed hard candy melts in the oven to give these beautiful cookies the look of stained glass. They're pretty enough to be hung on your tree.

ACTIVE TIME: 2 HOURS • **BAKE TIME:** 10 MINUTES PER BATCH
MAKES ABOUT 120 COOKIES

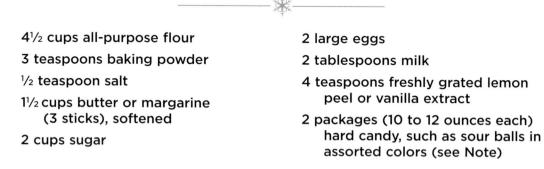

4½ cups all-purpose flour

3 teaspoons baking powder

½ teaspoon salt

1½ cups butter or margarine (3 sticks), softened

2 cups sugar

2 large eggs

2 tablespoons milk

4 teaspoons freshly grated lemon peel or vanilla extract

2 packages (10 to 12 ounces each) hard candy, such as sour balls in assorted colors (see Note)

1 • In large bowl, whisk flour, baking powder, and salt until blended. In separate large bowl, with mixer at medium speed, beat butter and 1½ cups sugar until light and fluffy. Beat in eggs, milk, and lemon peel or vanilla until well combined. Reduce speed to low; beat in flour mixture just until blended. Divide dough in half and shape each half into 2 balls; flatten each ball into a disk. Wrap each disk in plastic and refrigerate at least 2 hours or up to overnight.

2 • While dough is chilling, group candies by color and place in separate heavy-duty zip-tight plastic bags. Place 1 bag on towel-covered work surface. With meat mallet or rolling pin, lightly crush candy into small pieces, being careful not to crush until fine and powdery. Repeat with remaining candy.

3 • Preheat oven to 350°F. Line two large cookie sheets with foil. On lightly floured surface, with floured rolling pin, roll 1 disk of dough ⅛ inch thick; keep remaining dough refrigerated. With floured 3-inch assorted cookie cutters, cut dough into as many cookies as possible; reserve trimmings for rerolling. Place cut-out cookies on foil-lined sheets. With mini cookie cutters, canapé cutters, or knife, cut one or more small shapes from each large cookie; remove small cut-out pieces and reserve for rerolling. Place some crushed candy in cutouts of each cookie. If desired, with drinking straw, make a hole in top of each cookie for hanging.

4 • Bake until lightly browned, 10 to 12 minutes. Cool cookies completely on cookie sheets on wire racks. Repeat with remaining dough and trimmings.

5 • For wreath, tree, or window decorations, tie ribbons or nylon fishing line through hole in each cookie to make loop for hanging.

NOTE: Do not use red-and-white-swirled peppermint candies; they won't melt in the oven.

EACH COOKIE: About 90 calories, 1 g protein, 14 g carbohydrate, 4 g total fat (1 g saturated), 7 mg cholesterol, 40 mg sodium.

palmiers

These flaky pastries are a snap with our easy four-ingredient recipe. The dough can be shaped ahead and refrigerated for up to one week or frozen for up to three. Slice and bake when you're ready.

ACTIVE TIME: 35 MINUTES • **BAKE TIME:** 15 MINUTES PER BATCH • **MAKES** ABOUT 112 COOKIES

1½ cups butter (3 sticks), cut into pieces

3 cups all-purpose flour

¾ cup sour cream

1 cup sugar

1 • In large bowl, with pastry blender or two knives used scissor-fashion, cut butter into flour until mixture resembles course crumbs. Stir in sour cream. On lightly floured surface, knead dough just until it holds together; flatten into 8" by 6" rectangle. Wrap tightly in plastic wrap and refrigerate overnight.

2 • Preheat oven to 400°F. Sprinkle ½ cup sugar evenly over work surface. Cut dough in half. With lightly floured rolling pin, on sugared surface, roll 1 piece of dough into 14-inch square; keep remaining dough refrigerated. Using side of your hand, make indentation along center of dough. Starting from one side, tightly roll up dough to indentation. Roll up other side of dough until it meets first roll, incorporating as much sugar as possible into dough; refrigerate for 2 hours or up to 3 days. Repeat with remaining piece of dough and remaining ½ cup sugar.

3 • With serrated knife, cut one dough scroll crosswise into ¼-inch-thick slices. (Refrigerate if too soft to slice.) Place slices, 2 inches apart, on two ungreased large cookie sheets.

4 • Bake 10 minutes. With wide metal spatula, carefully turn cookies over. Rotate cookie sheets between upper and lower racks and bake until cookies are deep golden, about 5 minutes longer. Cool 1 minute on cookie sheets, then, with wide metal spatula, transfer cookies to wire racks to cool completely. Repeat slicing, baking, and cooling with remaining dough scroll.

EACH COOKIE: About 44 calories, 1 g protein, 4 g carbohydrate, 3 g total fat (2 g saturated), 7 mg cholesterol, 26 mg sodium.

ROLLING AND CUTTING PALMIERS: Roll up dough from each side of a 14-inch square to meet at a mark in the center. Incorporate as much sugar as possible as you roll.

Cut shaped dough crosswise in to ¼-inch-thick slices with a serrated knife. If the dough seems soft, chill it before cutting.

finska kakor

Finnish cakes is the translation for these rich and shortbreadlike cookies.
(Pictured on page 60.)

ACTIVE TIME: 1½ HOURS • **BAKE TIME:** 17 MINUTES PER BATCH • **MAKES** 128 COOKIES

2 cups blanched almonds

1¼ cups sugar

8 cups all-purpose flour

3 cups butter or margarine
(6 sticks), softened

4 teaspoons almond extract

2 egg whites, beaten

1 • In food processor with knife blade attached, process almonds with ¼ cup sugar until almonds are finely chopped; set aside.

2 • In large bowl, combine flour, butter, almond extract, and remaining 1 cup sugar. With hand, knead ingredients until well blended and mixture holds together.

3 • Preheat oven to 350°F. Divide dough into 4 equal pieces. On work surface, between 2 sheets of waxed paper, roll 1 piece of dough into 12" by 8" rectangle, keeping remaining dough refrigerated. With pastry brush, brush dough rectangle with some egg white. Sprinkle with one fourth of almond mixture. With rolling pin, gently press almonds into dough.

4 • Cut dough rectangle lengthwise into 8 strips. Cut each strip crosswise into 4 bars. With wide spatula, place bars, about ½ inch apart, on ungreased large cookie sheets.

5 • Bake bars until lightly browned, 17 to 20 minutes. Transfer to wire rack to cool. Repeat with remaining dough.

EACH BAR: About 85 calories, 1 g protein, 8 g carbohydrate, 5 g total fat (1 g saturated), 0 mg cholesterol, 60 mg sodium.

walnut horns

These lovely walnut-filled crescents are perfect with coffee or tea and make a delicious addition to any holiday party plate. (Pictured on page 60.)

ACTIVE TIME: 2 HOURS PLUS FREEZING AND COOLING
BAKE TIME: 20 MINUTES PER BATCH • **MAKES** 160 COOKIES

2 cups butter or margarine (4 sticks)

5 cups all-purpose flour

2 containers (8 ounces each) sour cream

2 large egg yolks

1½ cups sugar

1½ cups walnuts, finely chopped

3 teaspoons ground cinnamon

Confectioners' sugar for garnish

1 • In large bowl, with pastry blender or two knives used scissor-fashion, cut butter into flour until fine crumbs form. In cup, with fork, mix sour cream and egg yolk. Stir sour-cream mixture into flour mixture just until blended and dough comes away from side of bowl (dough will be sticky). Cover bowl with plastic wrap and freeze 1 hour, or until firm.

2 • Divide dough into 10 equal pieces. On lightly floured surface, shape each piece into a disk. Wrap each disk in plastic wrap and freeze at least 4 hours or overnight, until firm enough to roll.

3 • In small bowl, combine sugar, walnuts, and cinnamon. On sheet of lightly floured waxed paper, with floured rolling pin, roll 1 piece of dough into 12-inch round, keeping remaining dough refrigerated. Sprinkle dough with rounded ¼ cup walnut mixture; gently press into dough. With pastry wheel or sharp knife, cut dough into 16 equal wedges. Starting at curved edge, roll up each wedge, jelly-roll fashion. Place cookies, point side down, 1½ inches apart, on ungreased cookie sheets. Shape each into crescent.

4 • Preheat oven to 350°F. Bake cookies until golden, about 20 minutes. With wide spatula, transfer cookies to wire rack to cool. When cookies are cool, sprinkle with confectioners' sugar. Repeat with remaining dough, 1 piece at a time.

EACH COOKIE: About 55 calories, 1 g protein, 5 g carbohydrate, 4 g total fat (1 g saturated), 4 mg cholesterol, 30 mg sodium.

best linzer cookies

Actually mini linzer tarts, these pastry shop favorites require a little extra work, but they are guaranteed to win you kudos.

ACTIVE TIME: 2 HOURS PLUS CHILLING • **BAKE TIME:** 17 MINUTES PER BATCH
MAKES ABOUT 96 COOKIES

2 bags (8 ounces each) pecans
1 cup cornstarch
3 cups butter (6 sticks), softened
2⅔ cups confectioners' sugar
4 teaspoons vanilla extract

1½ teaspoons salt
2 large eggs
5½ cups all-purpose flour
1½ cups seedless red raspberry jam

1 • In food processor with knife blade attached, pulse pecans and cornstarch until pecans are finely ground.

2 • In large bowl, with mixer at low speed, beat butter and 2 cups confectioners' sugar until blended. Increase speed to high; beat until light and fluffy, about 3 minutes, occasionally scraping bowl with rubber spatula. At medium speed, beat in vanilla, salt, and eggs. Reduce speed to low; gradually beat in flour and pecan mixture just until blended, occasionally scraping bowl.

3 • Divide dough in half, then divide each half into 4 equal pieces; flatten each piece into a disk. Wrap each disk in plastic wrap and refrigerate until dough is firm enough to roll, 4 to 5 hours.

4 • Preheat oven to 325°F. Remove 1 disk of dough from refrigerator; if necessary, let stand 10 to 15 minutes at room temperature for easier rolling. On lightly floured surface, with floured rolling pin, roll dough ⅛ inch thick. With floured 2¼-inch fluted round, plain round, or holiday-shaped cookie cutter, cut dough into as many cookies as possible. With floured 1- to 1¼-inch fluted round, plain round, or holiday-shaped cookie cutter, cut out centers from half of cookies. Wrap and refrigerate trimmings. With lightly floured spatula, carefully place cookies, 1 inch apart, on ungreased large cookie sheets.

5 • Bake cookies until edges are lightly browned, 17 to 20 minutes. Transfer cookies to wire rack to cool. Repeat with remaining dough and trimmings.

6 • When cookies are cool, sprinkle remaining ⅔ cup confectioners' sugar through sieve over cookies with cut-out centers.

7 • In small bowl, stir jam with fork until smooth. Spread top of each whole cookie with scant measuring teaspoon jam; place cut-out cookies on top.

EACH COOKIE: About 115 calories, 1 g protein, 11 g carbohydrate, 8 g total fat (3 g saturated), 17 mg cholesterol, 80 mg sodium

whole-wheat sugar cookies

Using white whole-wheat flour (see page 14) adds healthy whole-grain goodness to this low-fat variation on the classic. If you like, dress them up using our decorating tips on pages 23–27.

ACTIVE TIME: 1 HOUR PLUS CHILLING AND COOLING • **BAKE TIME:** 10 MINUTES PER BATCH
MAKES ABOUT 144 COOKIES

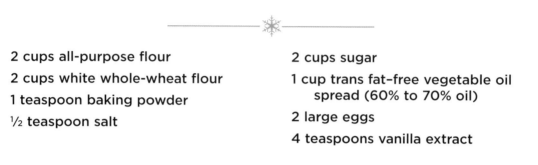

2 cups all-purpose flour

2 cups white whole-wheat flour

1 teaspoon baking powder

½ teaspoon salt

2 cups sugar

1 cup trans fat–free vegetable oil spread (60% to 70% oil)

2 large eggs

4 teaspoons vanilla extract

1 • In small bowl, whisk together all-purpose and whole-wheat flours, baking powder, and salt until blended.

2 • In large bowl, with mixer at low speed, beat sugar and vegetable oil spread until blended. Increase speed to high; beat until light and creamy, about 3 minutes, occasionally scraping bowl with rubber spatula. Reduce speed to low; beat in eggs and vanilla, then beat in flour mixture just until blended.

3 • Divide dough into 4 equal parts; flatten each into a disk. Wrap each disk with plastic wrap and refrigerate until dough is firm enough to roll, about 2 hours.

4 • Preheat oven to 375°F. On lightly floured surface, with floured rolling pin, roll 1 piece of dough ⅛ inch thick. With 2-inch cookie cutters, cut out as many cookies as possible; wrap and refrigerate trimmings. With lightly floured spatula, place cookies, 1 inch apart, on ungreased large cookie sheets. Repeat with second disk.

5 • Bake cookies until lightly browned, 10 to 12 minutes. With thin metal spatula, transfer cookies to wire rack to cool. Repeat with remaining dough and trimmings.

EACH COOKIE: About 35 calories, 1 g protein, 5 g carbohydrate, 1 g total fat (0 g saturated), 3 mg cholesterol, 20mg sodium

berry-orange linzer jewels

We've used our healthy Whole-Wheat Sugar Cookies recipe as the basis for this twist on the internationally popular Austrian pastry.

ACTIVE TIME: 1½ HOURS PLUS CHILLING AND COOLING • **BAKE TIME:** 10 MINUTES PER BATCH
MAKES ABOUT 108 LINZER COOKIES

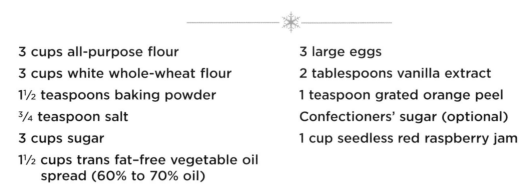

3 cups all-purpose flour

3 cups white whole-wheat flour

1½ teaspoons baking powder

¾ teaspoon salt

3 cups sugar

1½ cups trans fat–free vegetable oil
   spread (60% to 70% oil)

3 large eggs

2 tablespoons vanilla extract

1 teaspoon grated orange peel

Confectioners' sugar (optional)

1 cup seedless red raspberry jam

1 • Repeat steps 1 to 3 of whole-wheat sugar cookies (opposite).

4 • Preheat oven to 375°F. On lightly floured surface, with floured rolling pin, roll 1 piece of dough ⅛ inch thick. With scalloped 2-inch square or round cookie cutter, cut out as many cookies as possible. Using small star-shaped or other decorative cutter, cut out centers of half the cookies. Wrap and refrigerate trimmings. With lightly floured spatula, place cookies, 1 inch apart, on ungreased large cookie sheets. Repeat with second disk.

5 • Bake cookies until lightly browned, 10 to 12 minutes. With thin metal spatula, transfer cookies to wire rack to cool. Repeat with any remaining dough and trimmings.

6 • When cookies are cool, dust cookies with cut-out centers with confectioners' sugar, if you like. Spread flat side of each whole cookie with scant ½ teaspoon jam; top with cut-out cookie, flat side down.

EACH COOKIE: About 70 calories, 2 g protein, 10 g carbohydrate, 2 g total fat (0 g saturated), 6 mg cholesterol, 45 mg sodium

gingerbread cutouts

Kids of all ages love whimsical ginger people any time of the year. At Christmas this spicy dough is perfect for cutting into seasonal shapes or for constructing your own gingerbread house.

ACTIVE TIME: 1 HOUR PLUS COOLING AND DECORATING • **BAKE TIME:** 12 MINUTES PER BATCH
MAKES ABOUT 108 COOKIES

1½ cups sugar

1½ cups light (mild) molasses

4½ teaspoons ground ginger

3 teaspoons ground allspice

3 teaspoons ground cinnamon

3 teaspoons ground cloves

6 teaspoons baking soda

1½ cups butter or margarine (3 sticks), cut into pieces

3 large eggs, beaten

10½ cups all-purpose flour

Ornamental Frosting (optional, see page 25)

1 • In 3-quart saucepan, heat sugar, molasses, ginger, allspice, cinnamon, and cloves to boiling over medium heat, stirring occasionally with wooden spoon. Remove pan from heat; stir in baking soda (mixture will foam up in pan). Stir in butter until melted. Stir in eggs. Add flour and stir until dough forms.

2 • On floured surface, knead dough until combined. Divide dough into 6 equal pieces; wrap 5 pieces in waxed paper and refrigerate while working with remaining piece.

3 • Preheat oven to 325°F. On lightly floured surface, with floured rolling pin, roll 1 piece of dough until slightly less than ¼ inch thick. With floured 3- to 4-inch cookie cutters, cut dough into as many cookies as possible; reserve trimmings. Place cookies, 1 inch apart, on ungreased large cookie sheets.

4 • Bake until edges begin to brown, about 12 minutes. With wide metal spatula, transfer cookies to wire racks to cool. Repeat with remaining dough and trimmings.

5 • When cookies are cool, prepare Ornamental Frosting, if using, to decorate cookies; let set completely, about 1 hour.

EACH COOKIE WITHOUT FROSTING: About 95 calories, 2 g protein, 16 g carbohydrate, 3 g total fat (2 g saturated), 13 mg cholesterol, 100 mg sodium.

ALMOND MACAROON FINGERS (page 100)

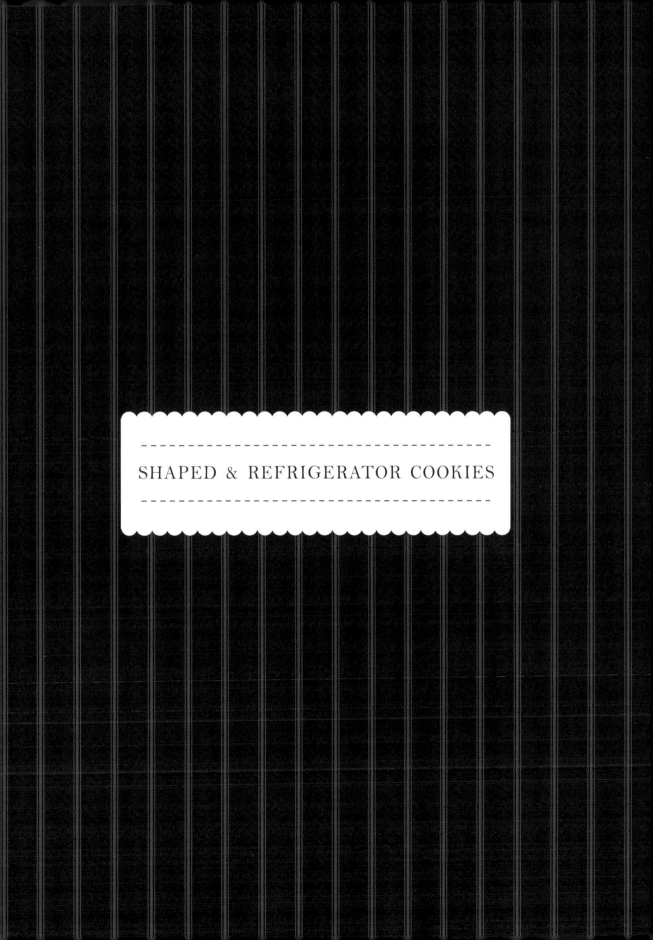

SHAPED & REFRIGERATOR COOKIES

WHETHER SHAPED, SLICED, CURLED, OR TWISTED, molded cookies are almost as much fun to make as they are to eat.

Refrigerator cookies, often called icebox cookies, became the "rage"—and the first convenience food—in the late nineteenth century, when women discovered that having a roll of cookie dough in the icebox meant they could serve warm cookies at a moment's notice. This time-saver is especially useful at cookie-swap time!

Follow these helpful suggestions for delicious results with every batch.

- Work quickly with each ball of dough. You can start shaping the dough as soon as it is made because molded cookie dough is usually stiff enough that it doesn't require chilling. But move fast so that the heat of your hands doesn't melt the butter in the dough and make it sticky.

- If the dough begins to stick to your hands, rubbing your hands with a little flour or vegetable oil will help.

- If the dough starts to get crumbly, moisten your hands with water. It will make the cookies easier to shape.

- Follow cookie press directions carefully, especially when making spritz cookies, as all of them have slightly different instructions.

- To freeze dough for refrigerator cookies just wrap it tightly in heavy-duty foil and pack in an air-tight container. It will keep frozen for three months. Be sure to thaw the dough in the refrigerator, and remember to label each package with the contents and date.

- To ensure even baking, rotate cookie sheets or pans between upper and lower oven racks halfway through baking.

snickerdoodles

Oringinating in New England, these cinnamon-sugar-coated butter cookies with the whimsical name, have a charactistically crackly surface. They are so much fun to make, the kids will beg to help.

ACTIVE TIME: 45 MINUTES • **BAKE TIME:** 12 MINUTES PER BATCH • **MAKES** ABOUT 108 COOKIES

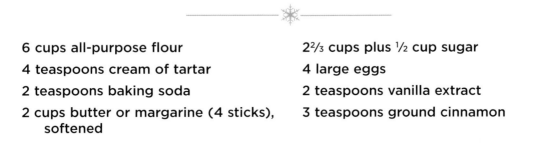

6 cups all-purpose flour

4 teaspoons cream of tartar

2 teaspoons baking soda

2 cups butter or margarine (4 sticks), softened

$2\frac{2}{3}$ cups plus ½ cup sugar

4 large eggs

2 teaspoons vanilla extract

3 teaspoons ground cinnamon

1 • Preheat oven to 375°F. In large bowl, whisk flour, cream of tartar, and baking soda.

2 • In separate large bowl, with mixer at medium speed, beat butter and $2\frac{2}{3}$ cups sugar until light and fluffy. Beat in eggs and vanilla. Reduce speed to low; beat in flour mixture until well blended.

3 • In small bowl, combine cinnamon and remaining ½ cup sugar. With hands, shape dough into 1-inch balls. Roll in cinnamon-sugar to coat. Place balls, 1 inch apart, on two ungreased large cookie sheets.

4 • Bake until set and lightly crinkly on top, 12 minutes. Cool on cookie sheets on wire racks 1 minute. With wide metal spatula, transfer cookies to wire racks to cool completely. Repeat with remaining dough.

EACH COOKIES: About 80 calories, 1 g protein, 11 g carbohydrate, 4 g total fat (2 g saturated), 17 mg cholesterol, 60 mg sodium.

mexican wedding cookies

You don't need a wedding as an excuse to make these delightful treats. They will be more than welcome at any cookie exchange.

ACTIVE TIME: 1 HOUR PLUS COOLING • **BAKE TIME:** 13 MINUTES PER BATCH
MAKES 96 COOKIES

———————— ❄ ————————

1⅓ cups pecans

3 tablespoons plus 1½ cups confectioners' sugar, sifted

2¾ cups all-purpose flour

¼ teaspoon of baking soda

¼ teaspoon salt

1 cup butter (2 sticks), softened (do not use margarine)

¾ cup granulated sugar

1 large egg

1 teaspoon vanilla extract

1 • In food processor with knife blade attached, pulse pecans with 3 tablespoons confectioners' sugar until very finely ground.

2 • In small bowl, whisk ground pecans, flour, baking soda, and salt until blended.

3 • In large bowl, with mixer at medium speed, beat butter and granulated sugar until creamy, about 1 minute, occasionally scraping bowl with rubber spatula. Add egg and vanilla; beat until well mixed. Reduce speed to low; gradually beat in flour mixture just until blended, occasionally scraping side of bowl.

4 • Preheat oven to 350°F. Shape dough by rounded measuring teaspoons into 1-inch balls. Place balls, 1½ inches apart, on two ungreased large cookie sheets.

5 • Bake until bottoms are browned and cookies are light golden, 13 to 15 minutes. Let stand on cookie sheets 2 minutes to firm up slightly, then transfer to wire rack to cool. Repeat with remaining dough.

6 • Place confectioners' sugar in pie plate. Roll cooled cookies in sugar to coat. Repeat if desired.

EACH COOKIE: About 60 calories, 1 g protein, 7 g carbohydrate, 3 g total fat, (1 g saturated), 8 mg cholesterol, 30mg sodium

cocoa wedding cookies

The addition of cocoa and chocolate chips gives this variation on Mexican Wedding Cookies (opposite) mass appeal. Be sure to roll the confectioners' sugar while they're still warm and again when they have cooled or just before serving.

ACTIVE TIME: 45 MINUTES PLUS COOLING• **BAKE TIME** 16 MINUTES PER BATCH
MAKES ABOUT 108 COOKIES

2 cups pecans

3½ cups confectioners' sugar

2 cups cold butter (4 sticks), cut into pieces (do not use margarine)

2 teaspoons vanilla extract

3½ cups all-purpose flour

⅔ cup unsweetened cocoa

⅔ cup semisweet chocolate mini-chips

1 • Preheat oven to 325°F.

2 • In food processor with knife blade attached, pulse pecans with 1 cup confectioners' sugar until pecans are finely ground. Add butter and vanilla and process until smooth, occasionally stopping processor to scrape side with rubber spatula. Add flour and cocoa and pulse until evenly mixed. Add chocolate chips; pulse just until combined.

3 • With floured hands, shape dough by rounded measuring teaspoons into 1-inch balls. Place balls, 1 inch apart, on 2 ungreased large cookie sheets.

4 • Bake cookies until bottoms are lightly browned, 16 to 18 minutes. Transfer cookies to wire rack to cool slightly.

5 • Sift remaining 1¼ cups confectioners' sugar onto waxed paper. While cookies are still warm, roll in sugar to coat; return to wire rack to cool completely. When cool, gently roll cookies in sugar again. Repeat with remaining dough and 1¼ cups sugar.

EACH COOKIE: About 80 calories, 1g protein, 8g carbohydrate, 6g total fat (3g saturated), 10mg cholesterol, 35mg sodium

chocolate crinkles

This cookie takes its name from its interesting shape. As the rich sugar-coated dough bakes, it spreads into puffy rounds with small furrows.

ACTIVE TIME: 45 MINUTES PLUS CHILLING • **BAKE TIME:** 8 MINUTES PER BATCH
MAKES ABOUT 96 COOKIES

1¾ cups all-purpose flour

½ cup unsweetened cocoa

1 teaspoon baking soda

½ teaspoon baking powder

¼ teaspoon salt

½ cup butter or margarine (1 stick), softened

1¼ cups granulated sugar

2 tablespoons light corn syrup

2 squares (2 ounces) unsweetened chocolate, melted and cooled

2 large eggs

2 tablespoons vanilla extract

½ cup confectioners' sugar

1 • In small bowl, whisk flour, cocoa, baking soda, baking powder, and salt until blended.

2 • In large bowl, with mixer at medium speed, beat butter, granulated sugar, and corn syrup until combined. Reduce speed to low; beat in chocolate, eggs, and vanilla until well blended. Beat in flour mixture until combined, scraping bowl occasionally with rubber spatula. Cover dough and refrigerate 1 hour.

3 • Preheat oven to 350°F. Place confectioners' sugar in small bowl. Shape dough by level measuring teaspoons into 1-inch balls; roll in confectioners' sugar.

4 • Place cookies, 1 inch apart, on ungreased large cookie sheets.

5 • Bake until set, about 8 minutes. With wide metal spatula, transfer cookies to wire racks to cool completely. Repeat with remaining dough and confectioners' sugar.

EACH COOKIE: About 35 calories, 1 g protein, 6 g carbohydrate, 1 g total fat (1 g saturated), 7 mg cholesterol, 35mg sodium.

spritz

Making these buttery molded favorites is quick and easy with modern cookie presses. You will find cookie-press patterns for every holiday, and this dough will work for all of them!

ACTIVE TIME: 15 MINUTES • **BAKE TIME:** 10 MINUTES PER BATCH • **MAKES** ABOUT 120 COOKIES

2 cups butter or margarine
(4 sticks), softened

1½ cups confectioners' sugar

2 teaspoons vanilla extract

¼ teaspoon almond extract

4 cups all-purpose flour

¼ teaspoon salt

1 • Preheat oven to 350°F. In large bowl, with mixer at medium speed, beat butter and confectioners' sugar until light and fluffy. Beat in vanilla and almond extracts. Reduce speed to low; add flour and salt and beat until well combined, occasionally scraping down bowl with rubber spatula.

2 • Spoon one-third of dough into cookie press fitted with pattern of choice. Press cookies, 1 inch apart, on two ungreased large cookie sheets.

3 • Bake until edges are golden brown, 10 to 12 minutes. With wide metal spatula, transfer cookies to wire racks to cool completely. Repeat with remaining dough.

EACH COOKIE: About 48 calories, 0 g protein, 5 g carbohydrate, 3 g total fat (2 g saturated), 8 mg cholesterol, 36 mg sodium.

spumoni icebox cookies

Contrary to what their name implies, spumoni cookies are not made with ice cream; they only look as if they were. With the help of some red and green paste food coloring, they resemble the popular Italian frozen dessert.

ACTIVE TIME: 55 MINUTES PLUS CHILLING AND COOLING • **BAKE TIME:** 10 MINUTES PER BATCH • **MAKES** ABOUT 180 COOKIES

5½ cups all-purpose flour

1 teaspoon baking soda

¼ teaspoon salt

2 cups butter or margarine (4 sticks), softened

2 cups sugar

2 eggs

2 teaspoons almond extract

⅔ cup shelled pistachios, finely chopped (about ½ cups pistachios in shell)

green paste food coloring

⅔ cup red candied cherries, finely chopped

red paste food coloring

1 • Line two 9″ by 5″ loaf pans with plastic wrap, extending wrap over all four sides. In medium bowl, whisk flour, baking soda, and salt until blended.

2 • In large bowl, with mixer at medium speed, beat butter and sugar until light and fluffy, about 4 minutes, occasionally scraping bowl with rubber spatula. Add eggs and almond extract and beat until well blended. Reduce speed to low; beat in flour mixture just until blended, occasionally scraping bowl.

3 • Transfer 2 rounded cups plain dough to medium bowl; with spoon, stir in pistachios and enough green food coloring to tint dough bright green. In another bowl, place 2 rounded cups plain dough; stir in cherries and enough red food coloring to tint dough bright red.

4 • Divide pistachio dough in half. Pat 1 half onto bottom of each prepared pan; freeze 10 minutes. Pat half of remaining plain dough on top of each pistachio layer; freeze 10 minutes. Pat half of cherry dough on top of each plain layer. Cover pans with plastic wrap and refrigerate until dough is firm enough to slice, 4 hours or overnight.

5 • Preheat oven to 350°F. Remove dough from 1 pan; discard plastic wrap. With serrated knife, cut dough crosswise into ¼-inch-thick slices, then cut each slice crosswise into 3 cookies. Place cookies, 2 inches apart, on ungreased large cookie sheet.

6 • Bake cookies until firm and edges are golden brown, 10 to 12 minutes. Cool cookies on cookie sheet on wire rack 2 minutes. With wide spatula, carefully transfer cookies to rack to cool completely. Repeat with remaining dough.

EACH COOKIE: About 45 calories, 1 g protein, 6 g carbohydrate, 3 g total fat (1 g saturated), 8 mg cholesterol, 35 mg sodium.

sally ann cookies

These wonderful frosted molasses cookies, widely available in grocery stores in the 1960s, are spiked with coffee for richer flavor.

ACTIVE TIME: 1 HOUR 25 MINUTES PLUS FREEZING AND COOLING
BAKE TIME: 15 MINUTES PER BATCH • **MAKES** ABOUT 144 COOKIES

COOKIES

1 cup butter or margarine (2 sticks), softened

1½ cups sugar

5½ cups all-purpose flour

1 cup light molasses

½ cup cold strong coffee

2 teaspoons baking soda

2 teaspoons ground ginger

½ teaspoon ground nutmeg

½ teaspoon ground cloves

SALLY ANN FROSTING

1 cup granulated sugar

1 envelope unflavored gelatin

1 cup cold water

2 cups confectioners' sugar

½ teaspoon vanilla extract

holiday decors (optional)

1 • In large bowl, with mixer at low speed, beat butter and sugar until blended. Increase speed to high; beat until creamy. At low speed, beat in flour, molasses, coffee, baking soda, ginger, nutmeg, salt, and cloves until well blended. Cover bowl with plastic wrap and freeze until firm enough to handle, 1 hour.

2 • Divide dough into thirds. On lightly floured surface, shape each third into 12-inch-long log. Wrap each log in plastic and freeze until firm enough to slice, at least 4 hours or overnight.

3 • Preheat oven to 350°F. Grease 2 large cookie sheets. Cut 1 log crosswise into ¼-inch-thick slices. Place slices, 1½ inches apart, on prepared cookie sheets.

4 • Bake until cookies are set and edges are lightly browned, 15 to 20 minutes. Cool on cookie sheet on wire rack 1 minute. With wide metal spatula, transfer cookies to wire rack to cool completely. Repeat with remaining dough.

5 • When cookies are cool, prepare frosting: In 2-quart saucepan, whisk granulated sugar and gelatin until well blended. Stir in water; heat to boiling over high heat. Reduce heat to low; simmer, uncovered, 10 minutes.

6 • Into medium bowl, measure confectioners' sugar. With mixer at low speed, gradually add gelatin mixture to confectioners' sugar and beat until blended. Increase speed to high; beat until mixture is smooth and fluffy and has an easy spreading consistency, about 10 minutes. Beat in vanilla. Keep bowl covered with plastic wrap to prevent frosting from drying out. Makes about 1¼ cups of frosting.

7 • With small metal spatula or knife, spread frosting on cookies. If you like, sprinkle cookies with decors. Let stand until frosting is completely set, about 1 hour.

EACH COOKIE WITHOUT DECORS: About 55 calories, 0 g protein, 10 g carbohydrate, 1 g total fat (0 g saturated), 0 mg cholesterol, 40 mg sodium.

almond macaroon fingers

It's hard to believe that cookies as chewy and rich as our chocolate-brushed macaroons are also low in fat, but it's the truth. (Pictured on page 88.)

ACTIVE TIME: 1½ HOURS • **BAKE TIME:** 17 MINUTES PER BATCH • **MAKES** ABOUT 125 COOKIES

3 cans (7 to 8 ounces each) almond paste

1½ cups confectioners' sugar

6 large egg whites

1½ teaspoons vanilla extract

6 ounces (6 squares) bittersweet or semisweet chocolate, broken into pieces

1 • Preheat oven to 300°F. Line two cookie sheets with parchment.

2 • In food processor with knife blade attached, process almond paste and sugar until combined (a few small lumps will remain). Add egg whites and vanilla; pulse until well combined.

3 • Spoon one–third of batter into decorating bag fitted with ½-inch star tip. Pipe batter into 3-inch-long fingers, 1 inch apart, on prepared cookie sheets.

4 • Bake macaroons until edges start to turn golden brown, 17 to 19 minutes. Cool on cookie sheets on wire racks. Repeat with remaining batter.

5 • In microwave-safe cup, heat chocolate in microwave oven on High until soft and shiny, 1 minute. Remove from oven; stir until smooth. With pastry brush, brush chocolate on half of each macaroon; let set. Or refrigerate 5 minutes to set chocolate. Peel cookies from parchment.

EACH COOKIE: About 45 calories, 2 g protein, 7 g carbohydrate, 2 g total fat (0 g saturated), 4 mg cholesterol, 30 mg sodium.

noisettines

The cream cheese and butter-rich crust of these tartlets is filled with a hazelnut–brown sugar mixture that literally melts in your mouth. After you taste one, you may not want to swap.
(Pictured on page 60.)

ACTIVE TIME: 1½ HOURS PLUS CHILLING AND COOLING • **BAKE TIME:** 30 MINUTES PER BATCH
MAKES 96 COOKIES

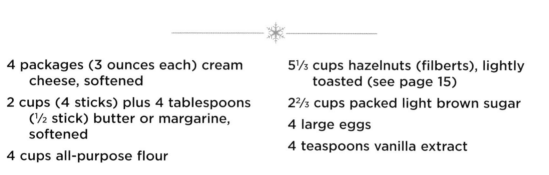

4 packages (3 ounces each) cream cheese, softened

2 cups (4 sticks) plus 4 tablespoons (½ stick) butter or margarine, softened

4 cups all-purpose flour

5⅓ cups hazelnuts (filberts), lightly toasted (see page 15)

2⅔ cups packed light brown sugar

4 large eggs

4 teaspoons vanilla extract

1 • In extra-large bowl, with mixer at high speed, beat cream cheese and 2 cups butter until creamy. Reduce speed to low; add flour and beat until well combined, occasionally scraping bowl with rubber spatula. Cover bowl with plastic wrap and refrigerate 30 minutes.

2 • Preheat oven to 350°F. Reserve 96 hazelnuts for garnish. In food processor with knife blade attached, process remaining hazelnuts with brown sugar until nuts are finely ground.

3 • In medium bowl, with spoon, combine hazelnut mixture, eggs, vanilla, and remaining 4 tablespoons butter.

4 • With floured hands, divide chilled dough into 96 equal pieces (dough will be very soft). Working with 24 pieces at a time, gently press each piece of dough evenly onto bottom and up sides of ungreased miniature muffin-pan cups. Spoon a heaping teaspoon hazelnut filling into each pastry cup; place 1 whole hazelnut on top of filling in each cup.

5 • Bake until filling is set and crust is golden, 30 minutes. With tip of knife, loosen cookie cups from muffin-pan cups and place on wire racks to cool completely. Repeat with remaining dough, hazelnut filling, and whole hazelnuts.

EACH COOKIE: About 135 calories, 2 g protein, 11 g carbohydrate, 10 g total fat (2 g saturated), 13 mg cholesterol, 75 mg sodium.

lemon slices

No one can pass up these old-fashioned thin lemon cookies we loved as children. For an elegant addition to your swap selection, sandwich them with lemon frosting or melted bittersweet chocolate.

ACTIVE TIME: 1 HOUR PLUS CHILLING • **BAKE TIME:** 12 MINUTES PER BATCH
MAKES ABOUT 96 COOKIES

4 cups all-purpose flour

1/2 teaspoon baking powder

1/2 teaspoon salt

4 to 6 large lemons

1 1/2 cups butter or margarine (3 sticks), softened

1 1/4 cups granulated sugar

1 cup confectioners' sugar

1 teaspoon vanilla extract

1 • In large bowl, whisk flour, baking powder, and salt until blended. From lemons, grate 2 tablespoons peel and squeeze 1/4 cup juice.

2 • In large bowl, with mixer at medium speed, beat butter, 1 cup granulated sugar, and confectioners' sugar until creamy. Beat in lemon peel and juice and vanilla until blended. Reduce speed to low; beat in flour mixture just until combined.

3 • Divide dough into 4 equal pieces. Shape each piece into 6-inch-long log. Wrap each log in waxed paper and refrigerate overnight. (If using margarine, freeze overnight.)

4 • Preheat oven to 350°F. Cut 1 log crosswise into scant 1/4-inch-thick slices; keep remaining logs refrigerated. Place slices, 1 1/2 inches apart, on two ungreased large cookie sheets. Sprinkle slices lightly with some of remaining 1/4 cup granulated sugar.

5 • Bake until edges are lightly browned, 12 minutes. Cool on cookie sheets on wire racks 2 minutes. With wide metal spatula, transfer cookies to wire racks to cool completely. Repeat with remaining dough and granulated sugar.

EACH COOKIE: About 63 calories, 1 g protein, 8 g carbohydrate, 3 g total fat (1 g saturated), 8 mg cholesterol, 44 mg sodium.

citrus slices

For an icebox sugar cookie that's a little different, exercise your decorating skills on these pretty trompe l'oeil lemon, orange, and lime slices.

ACTIVE TIME: 2 HOURS PLUS CHILLING AND COOLING • **BAKE TIME:** 10 MINUTES PER BATCH
MAKES ABOUT 168 COOKIES

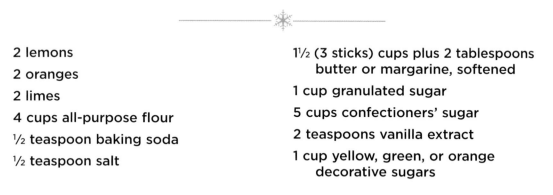

2 lemons

2 oranges

2 limes

4 cups all-purpose flour

½ teaspoon baking soda

½ teaspoon salt

1½ (3 sticks) cups plus 2 tablespoons butter or margarine, softened

1 cup granulated sugar

5 cups confectioners' sugar

2 teaspoons vanilla extract

1 cup yellow, green, or orange decorative sugars

1 • From lemons, grate 2 teaspoons peel and squeeze 2 tablespoons juice. From oranges, grate 2 teaspoons peel and squeeze 4 tablespoons juice. From limes, grate 2 teaspoons peel and squeeze 4 tablespoons juice. Reserve lemon and orange juice for making citrus icing.

2 • In medium bowl, whisk flour, baking soda, and salt until blended. In large bowl, with mixer at medium speed, beat 1½ cups butter, granulated sugar, and 1 cup confectioners' sugar until creamy, scraping bowl often with rubber spatula. Reduce speed to low; beat in citrus peels, lime juice, and 1 teaspoon vanilla until mixed. Gradually beat in flour mixture just until blended.

3 • With floured hands, divide dough into 4 equal pieces, Shape each piece into 8-inch-long log. Wrap each log in plastic wrap and refrigerate until dough is firm enough to slice, at least 4 hours or overnight. (Or place dough in freezer 1 hour.)

4 • Preheat oven to 350°F. Working with 1 log at a time, remove dough from refrigerator and unwrap. With sharp knife, cut log crosswise into scant ¼-inch-thick slices. Place slices, 2 inches apart, on two ungreased large cookie sheets. Sprinkle slices with choice of colored sugar. Shake off excess sugar from cookie sheet onto waxed paper; reuse if you like. Repeat with another log and separate cookie sheets.

5 • Bake until edges are golden, 10 to 12 minutes. Transfer cookies to wire racks to cool. Repeat with remaining logs.

6 • When cookies are cool, prepare citrus icing: In medium microwave-safe bowl, melt remaining 2 tablespoons butter in microwave oven on High, about 1 minute; cool. Add remaining 4 cups confectioners' sugar, 1 teaspoon vanilla, and reserved lemon and orange juice to melted butter and whisk until blended. Fill decorating bag fitted with small writing tip with citrus icing; use to pipe lines on cookies to resemble membranes on a citrus slice and small teardrops to resemble seeds. Allow icing to set completely, about 1 hour.

EACH COOKIE: About 50 calories, 0 g protein, 8 g carbohydrate, 2 g total fat (1 g saturated), 5 mg cholesterol, 30 mg sodium.

REFRIGERATOR COOKIES: Shape the dough roughly into a log, then use the waxed paper to roll and smooth it into a cylinder of even thickness.

As you slice the log of dough, turn it every few cuts so that the bottom doesn't become flattened.

angeletti

With a cookie as light as a cloud and a glaze as white as angel's wings, it's no wonder these cakelike rounds are standard features in most Italian pastry shops—and a sure bet they'll be a hit at your holiday swap as well.

ACTIVE TIME: 40 MINUTES PLUS COOLING • **BAKE TIME:** 7 MINUTES PER BATCH
MAKES ABOUT 120 COOKIES

1 cup butter or margarine (2 sticks), melted and cooled

1½ cups granulated sugar

½ cup whole milk

3 teaspoons vanilla extract

6 large eggs

6 cups all-purpose flour

2 tablespoons baking powder

½ teaspoon salt

4 cups confectioners' sugar

9 tablespoons water

1 cup multicolor candy decors

1 • Preheat oven to 375°F. Grease two large cookie sheets.

2 • In large bowl, whisk butter, granulated sugar, milk, vanilla, and eggs until blended. In medium bowl, mix flour, baking powder, and salt. Stir flour mixture into egg mixture until evenly blended. Cover dough with plastic wrap or waxed paper; let stand 5 minutes.

3 • With floured hands, shape dough by level tablespoons into 1-inch balls. Place balls, 2 inches apart, on prepared cookie sheets.

4 • Bake cookies until puffed and light brown on bottoms, 7 to 8 minutes. With wide metal spatula, transfer cookies to wire racks to cool. Repeat with remaining dough.

5 • When cookies are cool, in small bowl, whisk confectioners' sugar and water until blended. Dip top of each cookie into glaze. Place cookies on wire racks set over waxed paper to catch any drips. Immediately sprinkle cookies with decors. Allow glaze to set, about 20 minutes.

EACH COOKIE: About 75 calories, 1 g protein, 13 g carbohydrate, 2 g total fat (1 g saturated), 15 mg cholesterol, 55 mg sodium.

nut crescents

There are many variations of these buttery, ground-nut cookies, but this one is our favorite. Lightly toasting the almonds or hazelnuts intensifies the nutty flavor. (Pictured on page 111.)

ACTIVE TIME: 1 HOUR • **BAKE TIME:** 20 MINUTES PER BATCH • **MAKES** ABOUT 144 COOKIES

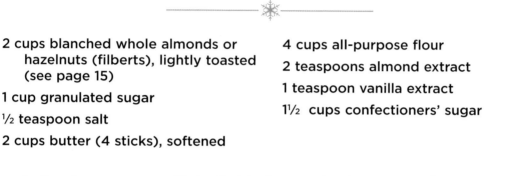

2 cups blanched whole almonds or hazelnuts (filberts), lightly toasted (see page 15)

1 cup granulated sugar

½ teaspoon salt

2 cups butter (4 sticks), softened

4 cups all-purpose flour

2 teaspoons almond extract

1 teaspoon vanilla extract

1½ cups confectioners' sugar

1 • In food processor with knife blade attached, process almonds, ½ cup granulated sugar, and salt until almonds are very finely ground.

2 • In large bowl, with mixer at low speed, beat butter and remaining ½ cup granulated sugar until blended, occasionally scraping bowl with rubber spatula. Increase speed to high; beat until light and fluffy, about 3 minutes. Reduce speed to low. Gradually add flour, ground-almond mixture, and almond and vanilla extracts; beat until blended.

3 • Divide dough into 4 equal pieces. Wrap each piece in plastic wrap and refrigerate until dough is firm enough to handle, about 1 hour, or freeze about 30 minutes.

4 • Preheat oven to 325°F. Working with 1 piece of dough at a time, with lightly floured hands, shape rounded teaspoons of dough into 2" by ½" crescents. Place crescents, 1 inch apart, on two ungreased cookie sheets.

5 • Bake until edges are lightly browned, about 20 minutes. With wide metal spatula, transfer cookies to wire racks set over waxed paper. Immediately dust cookies with some confectioners' sugar until well coated; cool completely. Repeat with remaining dough.

EACH COOKIE: About 58 calories, 1 g protein, 6 g carbohydrate, 4 g total fat (2 g saturated), 7 mg cholesterol, 34 mg sodium.

pb+j thumbprints

Here's the perfect cookie if your cookie swap involves kids—especially if they are fond of PB+J sandwiches.

ACTIVE TIME: 1 HOUR PLUS COOLING • **BAKE TIME** 13 MINUTES PER BATCH
MAKES ABOUT 120 COOKIES

3 cups all-purpose flour

1 teaspoon baking powder

½ teaspoon baking soda

¼ teaspoon salt

1 cup butter or margarine
(2 sticks), softened

1 cup creamy peanut butter

1 cup packed brown sugar

½ cup granulated sugar

2 large eggs

2 tablespoons dark corn syrup

2 teaspoons vanilla extract

1⅓ cups dry-roasted peanuts,
finely chopped

½ cup strawberry jam.

1 • Preheat oven to 350°F. In medium bowl, whisk flour, baking powder, baking soda, and until blended.

2 • In large bowl, with mixer at medium speed, beat butter, peanut butter, and brown and granulated sugars until creamy, occasionally scraping bowl with rubber spatula. Add eggs, corn syrup, and vanilla; beat until well blended. Reduce speed to low; gradually beat in flour mixture just until blended, occasionally scraping bowl.

3 • On sheet of waxed paper, place peanuts. Shape dough by rounded measuring teaspoons into 1-inch balls; roll in peanuts. Place balls, 2 inches apart, on two ungreased large cookie sheets. With thumb or end of wooden spoon handle, make small indentation in center of each ball.

4 • Bake 8 minutes. Remove cookie sheets from oven and gently press each indentation again, then fill each with rounded ¼ teaspoon jam. Return to oven and bake until cookies are set and edges begin to brown lightly, 5 to 6 minutes longer. Transfer cookies to wire racks to cool. Repeat with remaining dough, peanuts, and jam.

EACH COOKIE: About 70 calories, 1 g protein, 9 g carbohydrate, 4 g total fat (1 g saturated), 8 mg cholesterol, 55 mg sodium.

raspberry linzer thumbprints

The inspiration for these charming cookies is the Linzertorte, a traditional dessert from the Austrian city of Linz. The elaborate torte features a rich nut crust, raspberry filling, and a lattice top. Much simpler to prepare, this hazelnut cookie dough is made in the food processor. Instead of raspberry jam you could use any favorite flavor.

ACTIVE TIME: 1 HOUR • **BAKE TIME:** 20 MINUTES PER BATCH • **MAKES** ABOUT 96 COOKIES

2⅔ cups hazelnuts (filberts), toasted (see page 115)

1 cup sugar

1½ cups butter or margarine (3 sticks), cut into pieces

2 teaspoons vanilla extract

½ teaspoon salt

3½ cups all-purpose flour

½ cup seedless red raspberry jam

1 • Preheat oven to 350°F.

2 • In food processor with knife blade attached, process toasted hazelnuts with sugar until nuts are finely ground. Add butter, vanilla, and salt and process until blended. Add flour and process until evenly combined. Remove knife blade and press dough together with hands.

3 • Finely chop remaining ⅔ cup hazelnuts; spread on sheet of waxed paper. With hands, shape dough, into 1-inch balls (dough may be slightly crumbly). Roll balls in nuts, gently pressing nuts onto dough to adhere. Place balls, about 1½ inches apart, on two ungreased large cookie sheets.

4 • With thumb, make small indentation in center of each ball. Fill each indentation with ¼ teaspoon jam.

5 • Bake until edges are lightly golden, about 20 minutes. With wide spatula, transfer cookies to wire racks to cool completely. Repeat with remaining dough and jam.

EACH COOKIE: About 75 calories, 1 g protein, 7 g carbohydrate, 5 g total fat (2 g saturated), 8 mg cholesterol, 40 mg sodium.

Left: Raspberry Linzer Thumbprints; Right: Nut Cresents (page 108).

figgy thumbprints

This is not your ordinary thumbprint cookie. It's filled with an orange-, honey-, and spice-laced fig mixture and coated in toasted walnuts.

ACTIVE TIME: 1 HOUR 30 MINUTES PLUS CHILLING AND COOLING • **BAKE TIME** 20 MINUTES PER BATCH • **MAKES** ABOUT 180 COOKIES

---❄---

COOKIE DOUGH

8 cups all-purpose flour

2 teaspoons salt

3 cups butter (6 sticks), softened

1½ cups granulated sugar

1½ cups packed dark brown sugar

4 teaspoons vanilla extract

6 large eggs

COATING

6 cups walnuts (24 ounces), toasted (see page 15)

4 large egg whites

FIG FILLING

4 large oranges

2 packages (11 ounces each) Calimyrna figs, stems discarded

4 tablespoons honey

1 teaspoon ground cinnamon

½ teaspoon ground allspice

1 • Prepare dough: In medium bowl, whisk together flour and salt until blended. In large bowl, with mixer at medium speed, beat butter and granulated and brown sugars until creamy, occasionally scraping bowl with rubber spatula. Reduce speed to low; beat in vanilla. Add eggs, one at a time, beating well after each addition. Gradually beat in flour mixture just until blended, occasionally scraping bowl.

2 • Divide dough in half, then divide each half into 4 equal pieces; flatten each piece into a disk. Wrap each disk with plastic wrap and refrigerate at least 2 hours or until dough is firm enough to shape. (Or place dough in freezer for 30 minutes.)

3 • Meanwhile, prepare coating: In food processor with knife blade attached, pulse walnuts until finely chopped. Spread nuts on sheet of waxed paper. In bowl or pie plate, with fork, beat egg whites slightly.

4 • Prepare filling: From oranges, grate 1 teaspoon peel and squeeze 1½ cups juice. In same food processor with knife blade attached, pulse figs until coarsely chopped. Add orange peel and juice, honey, cinnamon, and allspice and process until almost smooth, stopping processor occasionally and scraping side with rubber spatula. Transfer mixture to small bowl.

5 • Preheat oven to 350°F. Remove 1 piece of dough from refrigerator; shape by rounded teaspoons into 1-inch balls. Roll each ball first in beaten whites, then in walnuts, gently pressing nuts into dough. Place balls, 2 inches apart, on ungreased large cookie sheet. With finger, gently press each ball into a 1¾-inch round. With thumb or end of wooden spoon handle, make small indentation in center of each round. Repeat with another piece of dough on separate cookie sheet.

6 • Bake 10 minutes. Working quickly, remove cookie sheets from oven and gently press each indentation again, then fill each cookie with a rounded ½ teaspoon filling. Return to oven and bake until golden, 10 minutes longer. Transfer cookies to wire rack to cool completely. Repeat with remaining dough, coating, and filling.

EACH COOKIE: About 105 calories, 2 g protein, 11 g carbohydrate, 6 g total fat (2 g saturated), 16 mg cholesterol, 65 mg sodium.

peppermint meringues

Be sure to check your oven temperature. The meringues must bake slowly so that they become dry inside without browning on the outside.

ACTIVE TIME: 45 MINUTES PLUS DRYING AND COOLING • **BAKE TIME:** 2 HOURS PER BATCH
MAKES ABOUT 108 MERINGUES

8 large egg whites
½ teaspoon cream of tartar
2 cups confectioners' sugar

½ teaspoon peppermint extract (see Note)
Red and green food coloring

1 • Preheat oven to 225°F. Line two large cookie sheets with parchment.

2 • In large bowl, with mixer at high speed, beat egg whites and cream of tartar until soft peaks form when beaters are lifted. Gradually sprinkle in sugar, beating until meringue stands in stiff, glossy peaks. Beat in extract.

3 • Transfer half of meringue mixture to another bowl. Add enough red food coloring to one bowl of meringue to tint it a pale red. Add enough green food coloring to remaining meringue to tint it a pale green.

4 • Spoon red meringue into large zip-tight plastic bag; cut ¼-inch from corner. Repeat with green meringue in separate bag. Fit large decorating bag (we used a 14-inch bag) with basket-weave or large round tip (½-inch- or ¾-inch-diameter opening). Place decorating bag in 2-cup glass measuring cup to stabilize bag; fold top third of bag over top of cup to keep top of bag clean. Simultaneously, squeeze meringues from both plastic bags into decorating bag, filling it two-thirds full.

5 • Pipe meringue onto prepared cookie sheets, leaving 1 inch between each meringue. If using basket-weave tip, pipe 3- to 4-inch-long pleated ribbons; if using round tip, pipe 2-inch rounds.

6 • Bake meringues 2 hours. Turn oven off. Leave meringues in oven 30 minutes to dry. Remove meringues from oven. Turn oven temperature back to 225°F. Cool meringues completely. Remove from foil with wide metal spatula.

NOTE: Do not use extract containing peppermint oil; it will deflate meringue mixture. Imitation peppermint extract works well.

EACH MERINGUE: About 10 calories, 0 g protein, 2 g carbohydrate, 0 g total fat, 0 mg cholesterol, 5 mg sodium.

lemon meringue drops

Made with meringue and freshly grated lemon peel, these cookies will wow anyone—especially those who love lemon meringue pie.

ACTIVE TIME: 45 MINUTES PLUS DRYING AND COOLING • **BAKE TIME:** 1 HOUR 30 MINUTES PER BATCH • **MAKES** ABOUT 120 COOKIES

6 large egg whites

½ teaspoon cream of tartar

¼ teaspoon salt

1 cup sugar

4 teaspoons freshly grated lemon peel

1 • Preheat oven to 200°F. Line two large cookie sheets with parchment.

2 • In medium bowl, with mixer at high speed, beat egg whites, cream of tartar, and salt until soft peaks form when beaters are lifted. With mixer running, gradually sprinkle in sugar, 2 tablespoons at a time, beating until sugar dissolves and meringue stands in stiff, glossy peaks when beaters are lifted. Gently fold in lemon peel.

3 • Spoon meringue into decorating bag fitted with ½-inch star tip. Pipe meringue into 1½-inch stars, about 1 inch apart, on prepared cookie sheets.

4 • Bake meringues until crisp but not brown, 1 hour 30 minutes, rotating cookie sheets between upper and lower racks halfway through baking. Turn oven off; leave meringues in oven until dry, about 1 hour longer. Remove meringues from oven. Turn oven temperature back to 200°F. Repeat with remaining meringue.

5 • Cool meringues completely. Remove from parchment with wide metal spatula. Store in tightly covered container at room temperature up to 1 month.

EACH COOKIE: About 5 calories, 0 g protein, 2 g carbohydrate, 0 g total fat, 0 mg cholesterol, 10 mg sodium.

sugar twists

Simple, elegant, and oh-so-buttery good, these classic cookies will lend an air of sophistication to the cookie swap selections.

ACTIVE TIME: 1½ HOURS PLUS CHILLING AND COOLING • **BAKE TIME:** 11 MINUTES PER BATCH
MAKES ABOUT 108 COOKIES

3⅓ cups all-purpose flour

½ teaspoon baking soda

½ teaspoon salt

4 large eggs

1½ cups granulated sugar

1 cup butter (2 sticks), softened

2 teaspoons vanilla extract

White sugar crystals (optional)

1 • In small bowl, whisk flour, baking soda, and salt until blended. Separate 2 eggs, placing yolks in small bowl and whites in another. Cover and refrigerate whites; reserve for brushing on cookies.

2 • In large bowl, with mixer at medium speed, beat sugar and butter until creamy, occasionally scraping bowl with rubber spatula. Beat in whole eggs, egg yolks, and vanilla. Reduce speed to low; gradually beat in flour mixture until blended.

3 • Divide dough into 4 equal pieces. Wrap each piece in plastic wrap and refrigerate until dough is firm enough to roll, about 2 hours. Or place dough in freezer for 30 minutes.

4 • Preheat oven to 350°F. Grease two large cookie sheets.

5 • On lightly floured surface, with floured hands, press 1 piece of dough into 6″ by 3″ by ¾″ rectangle. (Keep remaining dough refrigerated.) Cut rectangle into 30 equal pieces; shape each piece into a 6-inch-long rope. Transfer 1 rope at a time to cookie sheet; gently shape into a loop, over-lapping ends (cookies will look like a ribbon). Repeat with remaining ropes, placing cookies 1 inch apart. Brush cookies with egg whites; sprinkle with sugar crystals, if you like.

6 • Bake cookies until lightly browned, 11 to 12 minutes. Transfer cookies to wire rack to cool. Repeat with remaining dough, egg whites, and sugar crystals.

EACH COOKIE: About 45 calories, 1 g protein, 6 g carbohydrate, 2 g total fat (1 g saturated), 13 mg cholesterol, 40 mg sodium.

christmas jewels

Loaded with candied fruits and pecans, these colorful treats look like mini slices of holiday fruitcake. The make-ahead dough logs can be kept in the fridge up to one week.

ACTIVE TIME: 1 HOUR PLUS CHILLING AND COOLING • **BAKE TIME:** 12 MINUTES PER BATCH • **MAKES** ABOUT 144 COOKIES

2 cups butter (4 sticks), softened

2 cups confectioners' sugar

2 large eggs

4½ cups all-purpose flour

1 teaspoon salt

⅔ cup red candied cherries

⅔ cup green candied cherries

⅔ cup diced candied pineapple

3 cups pecans

1 • In large bowl, with mixer at medium speed, beat butter and sugar until creamy, about 2 minutes, occasionally scraping bowl with rubber spatula. Reduce speed to low; beat in eggs until blended. Gradually beat in flour and salt just until combined, occasionally scraping bowl. With spoon, stir in candied fruits and 1 cup pecans.

2 • Cover bowl with plastic wrap and refrigerate dough at least 2 hours or until firm enough to shape. Meanwhile, finely chop remaining pecans.

3 • Divide dough into 4 equal pieces; shape each piece into 9" by 2" log. Spread one-fourth of chopped pecans lengthwise on 13-inch-long sheet of waxed paper. Roll 1 log in pecans, gently pressing to coat. Wrap log tightly in waxed paper. Repeat with remaining dough and pecans. Refrigerate logs until dough is firm enough to slice, about 3 hours or up to 1 week.

4 • Preheat oven to 350°F. Grease two large cookie sheets. Remove 2 logs from refrigerator; cut into scant ¼-inch-thick slices. Place slices, 1 inch apart, on prepared cookie sheets.

5 • Bake cookies until edges are golden, 12 to 13 minutes. Transfer cookies to wire racks to cool. Repeat with remaining dough.

EACH COOKIE: About 70 calories, 1 g protein, 7 g carbohydrate, 4 g total fat (2 g saturated), 10 mg cholesterol, 45 mg sodium.

scottish shortbread

Shortbread is always welcome, no matter the occasion. To streamline the process for turning out several batches, we recommend using six 8-inch round disposable baking pans so that you don't have to wait for one batch to cool before putting another in the oven.

ACTIVE TIME: 30 MINUTES PLUS COOLING • **BAKE TIME:** 40 MINUTES PER BATCH
MAKES 96 WEDGES

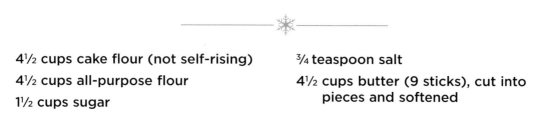

4½ cups cake flour (not self-rising)

4½ cups all-purpose flour

1½ cups sugar

¾ teaspoon salt

4½ cups butter (9 sticks), cut into pieces and softened

1 • Preheat oven to 325°F. In large bowl, whisk cake and all-purpose flours, sugar, and salt until blended. Knead butter into flour mixture until well blended and mixture holds together. (Or, in food processor with knife blade attached, pulse cake and all-purpose flours, sugar, and salt until blended. Add butter and pulse until mixture resembles coarse crumbs.)

2 • Divide dough into thirds, then divide each third in half. With hand, pat 1 piece onto bottom of each of six ungreased disposable 8-inch round cake pans. With fork, prick dough all over to make attractive pattern. Place three pans in the refrigerator.

3 • Bake three pans of shortbread until golden, about 40 minutes. Remove from oven; immediately run knife around edges of pans to loosen shortbread, then cut each round into 16 wedges. Cool completely in pans on wire racks. Repeat with remaining pans of dough.

4 • When cool, with small metal spatula, carefully remove cookies from pans.

EACH COOKIE: About 130 calories, 1 g protein, 12 g carbohydrate, 9 g total fat (5 g saturated), 23 mg cholesterol, 105 mg sodium.

greek cinnamon paximadia

Similar to biscotti, these sliced, crispy cookies are traditional Greek Christmas fare.

ACTIVE TIME: 1½ HOURS PLUS COOLING • **BAKE TIME:** 50 MINUTES PER BATCH
MAKES ABOUT 96 COOKIES

1 cup butter or margarine
  (2 sticks), softened

1 cup shortening

3 cups sugar

6 large eggs

2 tablespoons vanilla extract

4 tablespoons baking powder

1 teaspoon baking soda

About 8 cups all-purpose flour

3 teaspoons ground cinnamon

1 • In large bowl, with mixer at low speed, beat butter, shortening, and 2 cups sugar until blended. Increase speed to high; beat until light and fluffy, about 5 minutes. At low speed, add eggs, one at a time, beating well after each addition. Add vanilla; beat until well mixed.

2 • Gradually add baking powder, baking soda, and 7 cups flour and beat until well blended, occasionally scraping down side of bowl with rubber spatula. Stir in remaining 1 cup flour until soft dough forms. If necessary, add additional flour (up to ½ cup) until dough is easy to handle.

3 • Preheat oven to 350°F. Divide dough in half, then divide each half into 4 equal pieces. On lightly floured surface, shape each piece of dough into an 8-inch-long log. Place 2 logs, about 4 inches apart, on each of two ungreased large cookie sheets. Flatten each log to 2½-inch width.

4 • Bake logs until lightly browned and toothpick inserted in center comes out clean, about 20 minutes. Meanwhile, in pie plate, mix cinnamon and remaining 1 cup sugar.

5 • Remove cookie sheets from oven. Transfer hot loaves (during baking, logs will spread and become loaves) to cutting board. With serrated knife, cut each log diagonally into ½-inch-thick slices. Coat slices with cinnamon-sugar. Return slices, cut side down, to same cookie sheets. Bake slices 15 minutes. Turn slices over and bake until golden, 15 minutes longer. Transfer cookies to wire racks to cool. Repeat with remaining dough.

EACH COOKIE: About 105 calories, 1 g protein, 14 g carbohydrate, 5 g total fat (1 g saturated), 13 mg cholesterol, 60 mg sodium.

pistachio and cherry biscotti

Whether or not you dip these fruit-and-nut biscotti in chocolate, they're perfect for any cookie swap.

ACTIVE TIME: 1 HOUR 45 MINUTES PLUS COOLING • **BAKE TIME:** 40 MINUTES PER BATCH
MAKES ABOUT 96 BISCOTTI

———————— ❄ ————————

BISCOTTI

4 cups all-purpose flour

2 cups sugar

2 teaspoons baking powder

½ teaspoon salt

¼ teaspoon ground cinnamon

½ cup cold butter or margarine (½ stick), cut into pieces

6 large eggs, lightly beaten

2 cups dried tart cherries

2 cups shelled pistachios (about 16 ounces in shells), toasted (see page 15) and coarsely chopped

2 teaspoons vanilla extract

CHOCOLATE FOR DIPPING

12 ounces (12 squares) white chocolate, Swiss confectionary bar, or white baking bar, chopped

4 teaspoons vegetable shortening

1 • Preheat oven to 350°F. Prepare biscotti: In large bowl, whisk flour, sugar, baking powder, salt, and cinnamon until blended. With pastry blender or two knives used scissors-fashion, cut in butter until mixture resembles fine crumbs.

2 • Spoon 1 tablespoon beaten eggs into cup; reserve. Add cherries, pistachios, vanilla, and remaining beaten eggs to flour mixture; stir until evenly moistened. With hand, press dough together to form a ball.

3 • With floured hands, divide dough in half, then divide each half into 4 equal pieces. On each of 2 large ungreased cookie sheets, shape 2 pieces of dough, into 9″ by 2″ logs, 4 inches apart. Use pastry brush to coat tops and sides of logs with reserved egg.

4 • Bake logs 25 minutes. Cool logs on cookie sheets on wire racks 10 minutes.

5 • Place 1 log on cutting board. With serrated knife, cut warm log cross-wise on diagonal into ½-inch-thick slices. Place slices upright, at least ¼ inch apart, on same cookie sheet. Repeat with remaining log. Bake slices 15 minutes, rotating cookie sheets between upper and lower racks halfway through baking. Cool biscotti completely on cookie sheets on wire racks. (Biscotti will harden as they cool.) Repeat with remaining dough.

6 • Prepare chocolate for dipping: In small microwave-safe bowl, melt chocolate with shortening in microwave oven on High, about 1 ½ minutes, whisking mixture occasionally until smooth.

7 • With small metal spatula, spread half of 1 flat side of each biscotti with some white-chocolate mixture; place on wire rack, chocolate side up. Let biscotti stand at room temperature until chocolate has set, at least 1 hour.

Each biscotti: About 110 calories, 2 g protein, 16 g carbohydrate, 5 g total fat (2 g saturated), 20 mg cholesterol, 45 mg sodium.

ginger biscotti

Small chunks of crystallized ginger give these cookies a pleasant bite. Cool them completely, then pack into an air tight jar to keep them crisp.

ACTIVE TIME: 45 MINUTES PLUS COOLING • **BAKE TIME:** 50 MINUTES
MAKES ABOUT 96 COOKIES

❋

6 cups all-purpose flour

2 tablespoons ground ginger

4 teaspoons baking powder

1 teaspoon salt

1 cup butter or margarine (2 sticks), softened

1 cup granulated sugar

1 cup packed light brown sugar

6 large eggs

1 cup finely chopped crystallized ginger

1 • Preheat oven to 350°F. Grease two large cookie sheets. In medium bowl, whisk flour, ground ginger, baking powder, and salt until blended.

2 • In large bowl, with mixer at medium speed, beat butter and granulated and brown sugars until light and creamy. Beat in eggs, one at a time, beating well after each addition. Reduce speed to low; beat in flour mixture until combined. Stir in crystallized ginger.

3 • Divide dough into 4 equal pieces. Drop 1 portion of dough by spoonfuls down length of one side of prepared cookie sheet; repeat with another portion on other side of same sheet. With floured hands, shape each into 12-inch-long log, leaving about 3 inches between logs. Repeat with remaining 2 portions on remaining prepared sheet.

4 • Bake until toothpick inserted in center of logs comes out clean, 30 minutes. Cool logs on cookie sheets on wire racks 10 minutes.

5 • Transfer logs to cutting board. With serrated knife, cut each log crosswise on diagonal into ½-inch-thick slices. Place half of slices, cut side down, on two ungreased cookie sheets. Bake until golden, 20 minutes, turning slices over halfway through baking. With wide metal spatula, transfer biscotti to wire racks to cool completely. Repeat with remaining slices.

EACH COOKIE: About 90 calories, 1 g protein, 15 g carbohydrate, 3 g total fat, (2 g saturated), 21 mg cholesterol, 65 mg sodium.

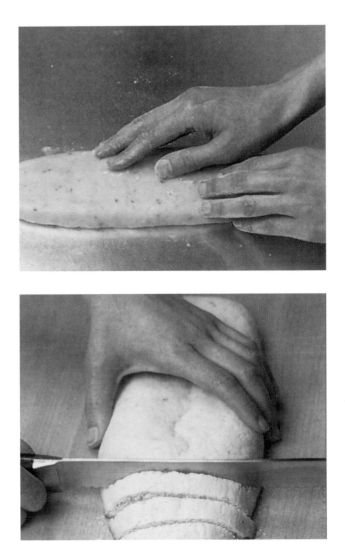

SHAPING BISCOTTI: Drop the dough by spoonfuls down the length of the cookie sheet. With lightly floured hands, flatten and shape it into a log of even thickness. After the first baking, slice the slightly cooled loaf with a serrated knife, using a gentle but confident sawing motion.

whole-grain gingersnaps

Without sacrificing taste or texture, we've made these gingersnaps a little healthier by replacing half of the all-purpose flour with whole-wheat flour and used trans fat–free vegetable oil spread.

ACTIVE TIME: 45 MINUTES PLUS CHILLING • **BAKE TIME:** 9 MINUTES PER BATCH
MAKES ABOUT 84 COOKIES

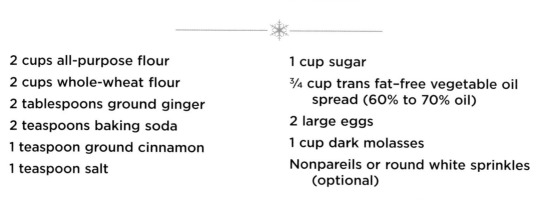

2 cups all-purpose flour

2 cups whole-wheat flour

2 tablespoons ground ginger

2 teaspoons baking soda

1 teaspoon ground cinnamon

1 teaspoon salt

1 cup sugar

¾ cup trans fat–free vegetable oil spread (60% to 70% oil)

2 large eggs

1 cup dark molasses

Nonpareils or round white sprinkles (optional)

1 • In medium bowl, whisk all-purpose and whole-wheat flours, ginger, baking soda, cinnamon, and salt until blended.

2 • In large bowl, with mixer on low speed, beat sugar and vegetable oil spread until blended. Increase speed to high; beat until light and creamy, occasionally scraping bowl with rubber spatula. Beat in eggs and molasses. Reduce speed to low; beat in flour mixture just until blended. Cover dough in bowl with plastic wrap and refrigerate until easier to handle (dough will still be slightly sticky), about 1 hour.

3 • Preheat oven to 350°F. With lightly greased hands, shape dough by heaping measuring teaspoons into 1-inch balls. If you like, dip top half of each ball in nonpareils. Place balls, 2½ inches apart, on two ungreased cookie sheets.

4 • Bake cookies until tops are slightly cracked, 9 to 11 minutes. (Cookies will be very soft.) Cool cookies on cookie sheets on wire racks 1 minute. With thin metal spatula, transfer cookies to rack to cool completely. Repeat with remaining dough.

EACH COOKIE: About 55 calories, 1 g protein, 9 g carbohydrate, 2 g total fat (0g saturated), 5 mg cholesterol, 75 mg sodium.

butterscotch fingers

Butterscotch—the magical combination of butter and brown sugar—
and pecans make these slice-and-bake cookies sure winners.

ACTIVE TIME: 30 MINUTES PLUS CHILLING • **BAKE TIME:** 12 MINUTES PER BATCH
MAKES ABOUT 96 COOKIES

———————————— ❄ ————————————

2⅓ cups all-purpose flour

½ teaspoon baking powder

½ teaspoon salt

1 cup butter or margarine
   (2 sticks), softened

1 cup packed dark brown sugar

1 teaspoon vanilla extract

1 large egg

¾ cup pecans, chopped

1 • In medium bowl, whisk flour, baking powder, and salt until blended.

2 • In large bowl, with mixer at medium speed, beat butter and sugar until blended, occasionally scraping bowl with rubber spatula. With wooden spoon, stir in pecans.

3• Shape dough into a 12" by 3¾" by 1" brick. Wrap brick tightly in plastic wrap and refrigerate until firm enough to slice, at least 6 hours or overnight. Or place brick in freezer for about 2 hours. (If using margarine, freeze brick overnight.)

4 • Preheat oven to 350°F. Grease large cookie sheet. With sharp knife, cut brick crosswise into ⅛-inch-thick slices. Place slices, 1 inch apart, on prepared cookie sheet.

5 • Bake until edges are lightly browned, 12 to 14 minutes. With wide metal spatula, transfer cookies to wire rack to cool. Repeat with remaining dough.

EACH COOKIE: About 45 calories, 1 g protein, 5 g carbohydrate, 3 g total fat (1 g saturated), 8 mg cholesterol, 38 mg sodium.

index

index

photo credits

Recipe For *

Recipe For *

Recipe For *

Recipe For *

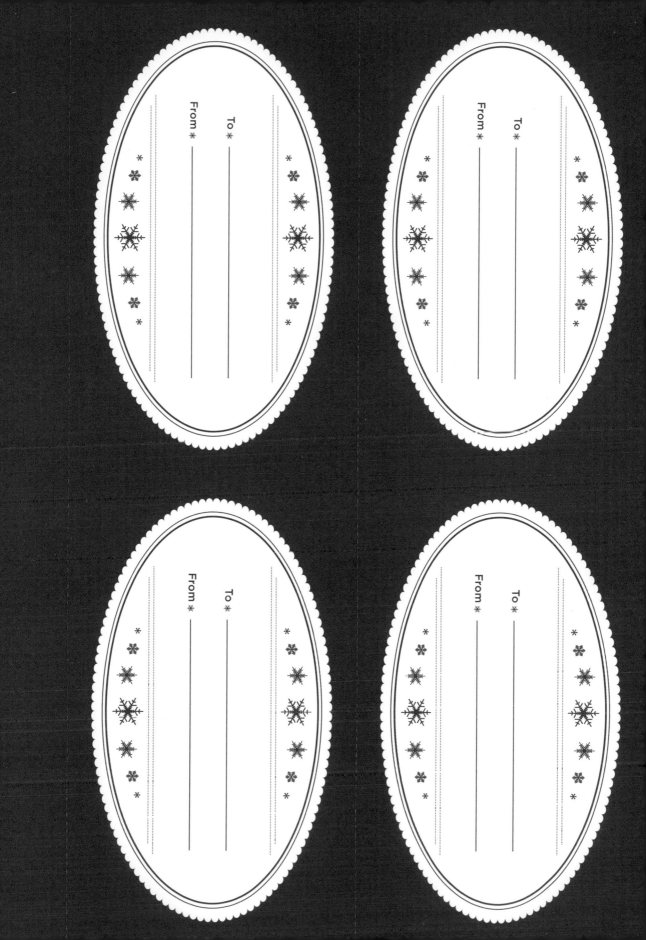

Recipe For ✳ _____

Recipe For ✳ _____

Recipe For ✳ _____

Recipe For ✳ _____

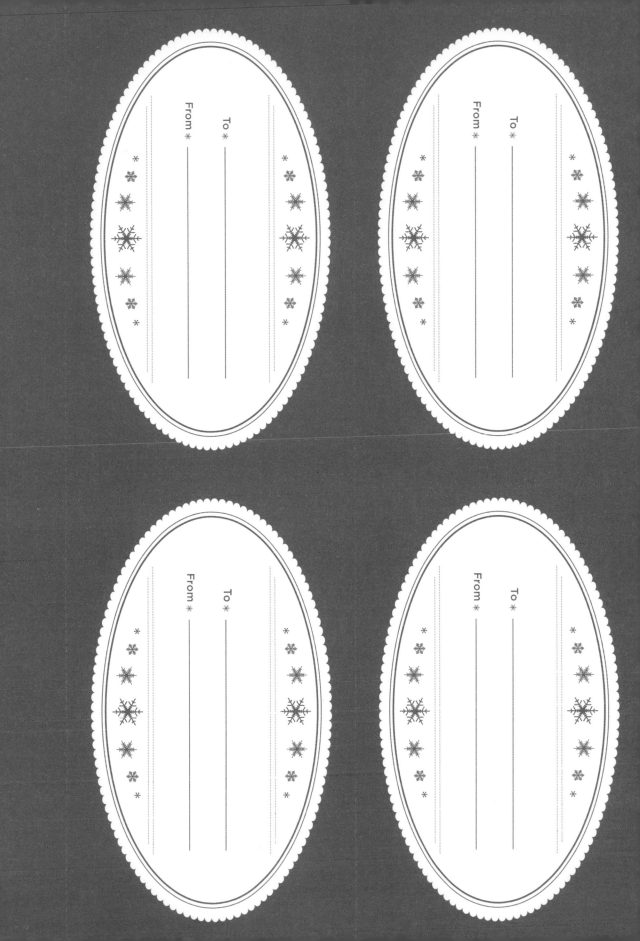

Recipe For ✳ _____

Recipe For ✳ _____

Recipe For ✳ _____

Recipe For ✳ _____

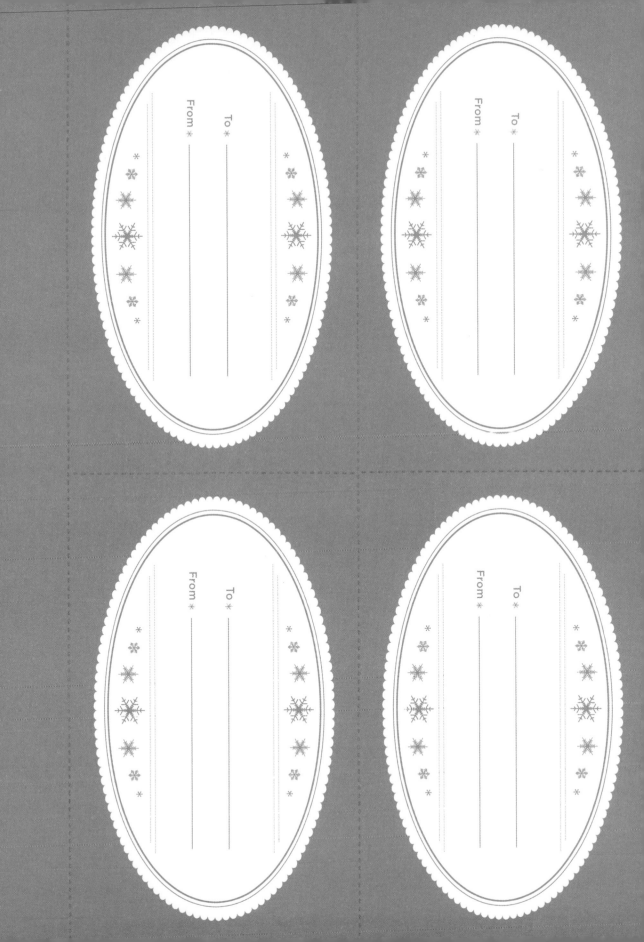

Recipe For ✳ _____

Recipe For ✳ _____

Recipe For ✳ _____

Recipe For ✳ _____

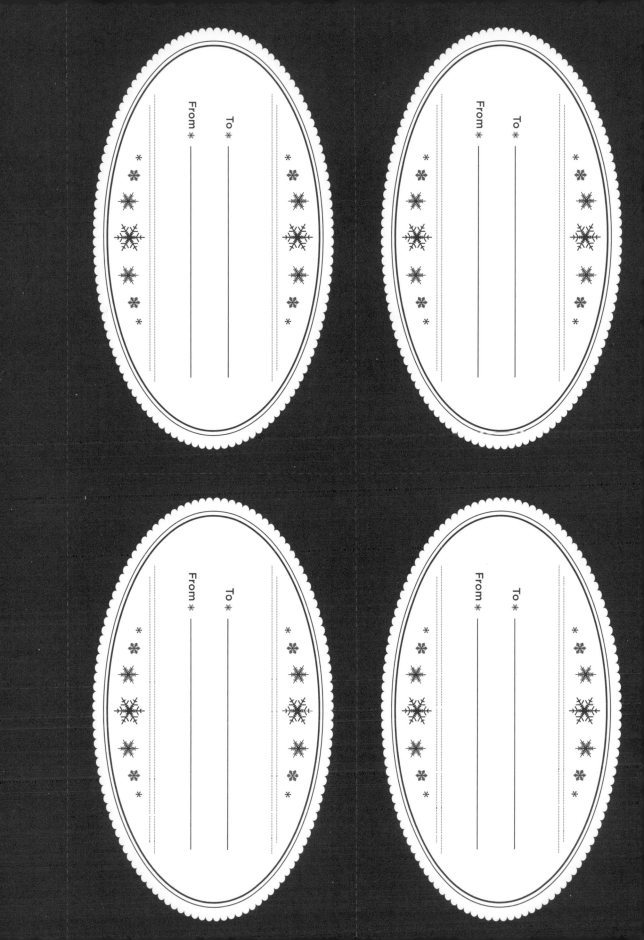

Recipe For ✳ _____

Recipe For ✳ _____

Recipe For ✳ _____

Recipe For ✳ _____

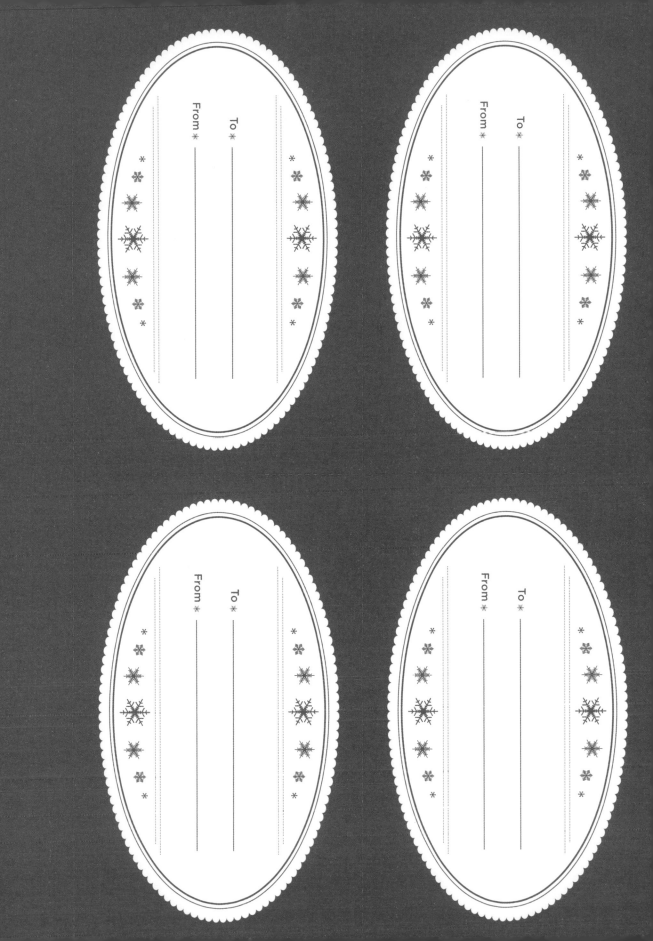

Recipe For ✳ _____

Recipe For ✳ _____

Recipe For ✳ _____

Recipe For ✳ _____

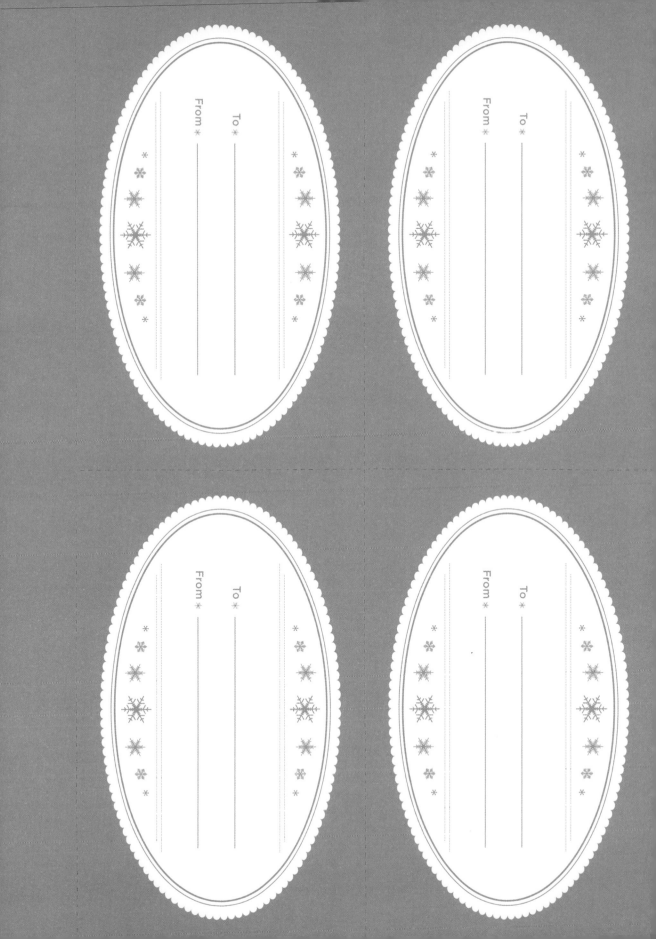

Recipe For ✳ _____

Recipe For ✳ _____

Recipe For ✳ _____

Recipe For ✳ _____

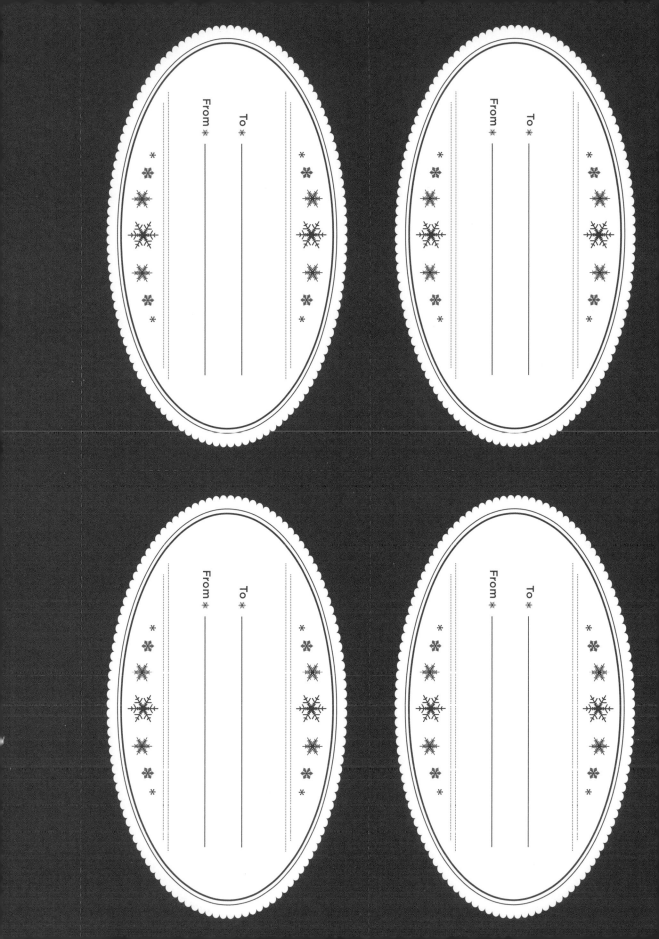

Recipe For ✳ _____

Recipe For ✳ _____

Recipe For ✳ _____

Recipe For ✳ _____